DAVID TUROFSKY   BEN FORD

WINGS AND THINGS

Lip-smacking chicken recipes

Photography by Dan Jones

Hardie Grant
QUADRILLE

CONTENTS

#StaySaucy

Everyone who loves chicken, loves chicken wings even more – is there anything better in the world? We don't think there is. No other type of food has as much of a cult following as the ever-humble but ever-so-delicious chicken wing. Having devoted thousands of hours to perfectly executing our favourite food, we put everything we have learnt into curating the multi-award-winning UK-based chicken concept: Wingmans.

What started as our joint love of wings turned into an obsession with homemade comfort food, fresh ingredients and game-changing flavours.

The concept of Wingmans first came about after David got back from living abroad in California as part of his university degree. It is fair to say, not much studying got done. The real education came from the varied and new food scenes within every city he travelled to. In comparison to traditional upmarket restaurants, this was fresh, vibrant and casual – the perfect mix.

David fell in love with the social dining elements of independent US BBQ shacks, burger bars and grills. Their knowledge and passion for the dishes they served along with the relaxed environment and friendly service was an experience he was not used to in the UK.

Meanwhile, Ben had been cooking for years and had always had a passion for no-fuss casual dining. Being able to eat great food in a chilled environment with good company, great music and laughter was the goal. After a quick phone call and a couple of beers, the idea of Wingmans was firmly implanted in our minds.

What started as our joint love of wings turned into an obsession with homemade comfort food, fresh ingredients and game-changing flavours.

In April 2015, after a couple of cooking sessions and little-to-no planning, we held a tasting day for our friends and family. Needless to say, bones were left clean. With bags of relentless enthusiasm we ventured into the world of street food and events. What awaited us were muddy fields, gazebos, sleepless nights, broken-down vans and poor trading days – also some great trading days and the biggest learning curve of our lives.

Four years on and having traded at some of the biggest events in the UK and across Europe, scooping us 12 different awards for our contribution to the glorious chicken wing, it was time to settle down and open our first bricks-and-mortar site. Supported by family and friends, we turned what was once a dream into a reality.

The recipes that follow are a mix of tried and tested dishes that are always crowd pleasers. There's something in here for everyone. Give it a try – after all, what's the worst that could happen? Some mistakes are the best inventions.

Be creative, stay saucy and get your wings on.

David & Ben

Get your wings on

Wings come in three parts: the tip, the drum and the flat. Depending on your preference, you can cook these whole or separate the drum and flat. Use the tips to make stocks and sauces.

Next is the cooking method – fried, smoked, grilled, BBQed or baked. From the most novice of cooks to the most experienced of chefs, there are recipes and techniques here for everyone.

It's important to choose the right oil for deep-frying. Rapeseed is good but pricier while vegetable oil is the most commonly available. Make sure your oil is fresh and fully preheated before you get cooking.

The most common and popular way to tenderize your wings is by marinating them in buttermilk. The addition of dry rubs, fresh herbs and citrus imparts flavour and really gets into the meat.

A floured coating is best when deep-frying wings but not necessary with other cooking methods. Seasoned flour or breadcrumbs add texture, flavour and all-important crunch to your wings.

Finally, make sure the wings are cooked through before eating. The best way to check is to insert a digital probe thermometer into the thickest part of the chicken and if it's 80°C then you are good to go.

Shanghai 2.0

While David was travelling around China, he fell in love with everything soy-based. So, obviously, when he came back we had to try to create something similar with wings; three batches, one hissy fit, and four kilos of wings later, Shanghai sauce was born. We entered this sauce at Wing Fest in the summer of 2016 and it hit all the right spots! Sweet, sticky, but super crunchy wings. It's still one of our bestselling wings to date, no matter whether it's in the restaurant or on the road.

In a large bowl combine the wings with the dry spices and the buttermilk. Let marinate in the fridge for at least 1 hour or up to 4 hours. Combine the two flours and set aside. Drain the wings from the excess marinade and toss through the flour – keep chilled until ready to cook.

Combine all of the sauce ingredients in a saucepan and bring to the boil. Once bubbling, remove from the heat and leave it to sit for as long as possible – this sauce is great if made the day before!

Preheat a deep fryer to 180°C (350°F). Place the wings in the basket and lower slowly into the fryer. Cook for 7 or 8 minutes, ensuring they hit 75°C (170°F) at the core of the thickest part of the wing and the juices run clear. If they don't hit 75°C (170°F) after the first 8 minutes just carry on cooking for a further minute.

To serve, toss the wings in enough sauce to coat them. Add the sesame seeds and toss again. Pile up on a plate or a basket. Drizzle with the Japanese mayo and finish with the red chilli, spring onions, ginger and top with the coriander.

SERVES 4

1.25kg (2lb 12oz) chicken wings, tip removed, drums and flat separated
1 Tbsp Chinese five spice
2 tsp celery salt
2 tsp white pepper
1 tsp black pepper
150ml (⅔ cup) buttermilk
250g (2½ cups) cornflour (cornstarch)
50g (⅓ cup) rice flour
2 or 3L (2 or 3qt) vegetable or rapeseed (canola) oil, for cooking

SAUCE

200ml (scant 1 cup) dark soy sauce
200ml (scant 1 cup) light soy sauce
100g (6 Tbsp) honey
100g (½ cup) soft dark brown sugar
50ml (¼ cup) sesame oil
100ml (scant ½ cup) rice vinegar or distilled vinegar
½ head of garlic, roughly chopped
50g (scant ½ cup) fresh root ginger, peeled and roughly chopped
Bunch of coriander (cilantro) stalks
Bunch of spring onions (scallions), roots removed and ends roughly chopped, green tops reserved for garnish

GARNISH

1 Tbsp black sesame seeds, toasted
1 Tbsp white sesame seeds, toasted
100ml (scant ½ cup) Japanese mayonnaise
1 fresh red chilli, finely sliced
Reserved green spring onion (scallion) tops, finely shredded
2 Tbsp finely chopped fresh root ginger
A few sprigs of fresh coriander (cilantro) or cress, chopped

A true Buffalo Wing needs to tick a few boxes to truly satisfy the lust that people have for this famous wing. Originating at the Anchor Bar in Buffalo, New York, these wings need to be super crispy when tossed in sauce. They should be buttery and spicy with just enough tang to keep you wanting to go in for another. This is our take on a classic. Made in New York; perfected in London!

Buffalo Wings

SERVES 4

1.25kg (2lb 12oz) chicken wings, tip
  removed, drums and flat separated
2 tsp celery salt
2 tsp white pepper
1 tsp black pepper
150ml (⅔ cup) buttermilk
250g (2½ cups) cornflour (cornstarch)
50g (⅓ cup) rice flour
2 or 3L (2 or 3qt) vegetable or rapeseed
  (canola) oil, for cooking
Buffalo Sauce (see page 175)
¼ bunch of fresh chives, chopped,
  to garnish

TO SERVE
4 celery sticks
Blue Cheese Sauce (see page 179)

In a large bowl combine the wings with the dry spices and the buttermilk. Let marinate in the fridge for at least 1 hour or up to 4 hours. Combine the two flours and set aside. Drain the wings from the excess marinade and toss through the flour – keep chilled until ready to cook.

Preheat a deep fryer to 180°C (350°F). Place the wings in the basket and lower slowly into the fryer. Cook for 7 or 8 minutes ensuring they hit 75°C (170°F) at the core of the thickest part of the wing and the juices run clear. If they don't hit 75°C (170°F) after the first 8 minutes just carry on cooking for a further minute.

As soon as the wings are cooked get them in a bowl and drench them in buffalo sauce. Stack them on a plate and sprinkle with the chives. Serve with the blue cheese sauce and celery sticks alongside.

Seoulja Boi

With the popularity of Korean fried chicken on the rise, it was time for us to develop a mind-blowing Korean-based hot sauce.

While we were developing this recipe, we always used a fiery gochujang base, but the addition of the roasted sesame dressing, pickled daikon, diced pineapple and lime to add sweetness into the mix was the icing on the cake. The Seoulja Boi became the winning Wild Wing entry at Wing Fest 2018 and one of our signature wings on our restaurant menus. Not only is it great for wings but we also recommend it as a burger sauce or a dressing.

In a large bowl combine the wings with the dry spices and the buttermilk. Let marinate in the fridge for at least 1 hour or up to 4 hours. Combine the two flours and set aside. Drain the wings from the excess marinade and toss through the flour – keep chilled until ready to cook.

For the seoulja boi sauce, spoon the gochujang into a small saucepan and add the soy sauce, vinegar, 150ml (⅔ cup) water and the sugar. Bring to a simmer. Once all the ingredients have combined together remove from the heat and stir in the sesame oil, seeds and garlic.

Preheat a deep fryer to 180°C (350°F). Place the wings in the basket and lower slowly into the fryer. Cook for 7 or 8 minutes ensuring they hit 75°C (170°F) at the core of the thickest part of the wing and the juices run clear. If they don't hit 75°C (170°F) after the first 8 minutes just carry on cooking for a further minute.

For the garnish, peel and core the pineapple. Dice the flesh and mix it with the sesame seeds and coriander. In a separate bowl, mix the daikon and red chilli. Grill the lime, cut sides down, on a very hot griddle pan until charred.

Either toss the wings in the sauce or dish them up and drizzle the roasted sesame dressing over the top, serving the sauce on the side. Sprinkle with the spring onions and serve with the daikon, pineapple and the charred lime.

SERVES 4

1.25kg (2lb 12oz) chicken wings, tip removed, drums and flat separated
2 tsp celery salt
2 tsp white pepper
1 tsp black pepper
150ml (⅔ cup) buttermilk
250g (2½ cups) cornflour (cornstarch)
50g (⅓ cup) rice flour
2 or 3L (2 or 3qt) vegetable or rapeseed (canola) oil, for cooking

SEOULJA BOI SAUCE

100g (½ cup) gochujang (red chilli paste)
200ml (scant 1 cup) light soy sauce
100ml (scant ½ cup) white vinegar
3 Tbsp caster (granulated) sugar
50ml (¼ cup) sesame oil
2 Tbsp black sesame seeds, toasted
2 Tbsp garlic granules

GARNISH

¼ fresh pineapple
1 Tbsp black sesame seeds, toasted
A few sprigs of fresh coriander (cilantro), finely chopped
100g (1 cup) pickled daikon, sliced
½ red chilli, very finely chopped
1 lime, halved
Roasted Sesame Dressing (see page 174)
Bunch of spring onions (scallions), green tops only, shredded

Ko Phan Bang

This sauce is no joke. The original Bang Coq has won over ten UK and European awards including Best of the Best at the British Street Food Awards from over 3,000+ vendors nationwide, and People's Choice at the European Awards from 19 countries, bringing home the gold for Team GB.

Best of all? It was an accident. It was the day before Wing Fest 2017 and we had no idea what to serve. We met up around midnight, two broken souls and covered in Buffalo sauce after a day of work. We had nothing but a load of sriracha, some dried goods and some fresh veggies David had grabbed on the way. After a beer and a brainstorm we had created a winner. It's a fiery Thai hot sauce infused with honey, and one of our most popular sauces!

In a large bowl combine the wings with the dry spices and the buttermilk. Let marinate in the fridge for at least 1 hour or up to 4 hours. Combine the two flours and set aside. Drain the wings from the excess marinade and toss through the flour – keep chilled until ready to cook.

Bruise the lemongrass and place in a saucepan with the lime leaves. Add the remaining sauce ingredients and bring to the boil. Allow to infuse for at least 1 hour or as long as you have.

Strain the sauce through a sieve. Adjust with a little extra seasoning or honey, if needed.

Preheat a deep fryer to 180°C (350°F). Place the wings in the basket and lower slowly into the fryer. Cook for 7 or 8 minutes ensuring they hit 75°C (170°F) at the core of the thickest part of the wing and the juices run clear. If they don't hit 75°C (170°F) after the first 8 minutes just carry on cooking for a further minute.

Add the crispy wings to a bowl and smother with sauce. Arrange in a serving bowl and spoon over some of the excess sauce. Drizzle with the mayonnaise and sprinkle over the ginger, coriander, sesame seeds and crispy onions and serve with quick pickled cucumber.

SERVES 4

1.25kg (2lb 12oz) chicken wings, tip removed, drums and flat separated
2 tsp celery salt
2 tsp white pepper
1 tsp black pepper
150ml (⅔ cup) buttermilk
250g (2½ cups) cornflour (cornstarch)
50g (⅓ cup) rice flour
2 or 3L (2 or 3qt) vegetable or rapeseed (canola) oil, for cooking

SAUCE

1 fresh lemongrass stalk
2 fresh kaffir lime leaves
3 Tbsp dark soy sauce
400ml (2 cups) sriracha
2 Tbsp sesame oil
100ml (scant ½ cup) white vinegar
200g (⅔ cup) honey, plus extra to taste
150g (¾ cup) caster (granulated) sugar
3 Tbsp freshly squeezed lime juice

GARNISH

100ml (scant ½ cup) Japanese mayonnaise
2 Tbsp finely chopped fresh root ginger
A few sprigs of fresh coriander (cilantro)
1 Tbsp white sesame seeds, toasted
50g (scant 1 cup) crispy onions
Quick Pickled Cucumber (see page 184)

Jamaican Heatwave

SERVES 4

1.25kg (2lb 12oz) chicken wings, tip removed, drums and flat separated
2 tsp celery salt
2 tsp white pepper
1 tsp black pepper
150ml (⅔ cup) buttermilk
250g (2½ cups) cornflour (cornstarch)
50g (⅓ cup) rice flour
2 or 3L (2 or 3qt) vegetable or rapeseed (canola) oil, for cooking

SAUCE

300g (10½oz) fresh red Scotch bonnet chillies, stems removed (wear gloves, these are seriously hot!)
1 white onion, finely chopped
1 carrot, thinly sliced
Walnut-sized piece of fresh root ginger, peeled and thinly chopped
1 beef tomato, finely chopped
2 garlic cloves, finely chopped
100ml (scant ½ cup) white vinegar
3 Tbsp caster (granulated) sugar
¼ bunch of fresh coriander (cilantro), chopped
¼ bunch of fresh mint, chopped

GARNISH

2 fresh red chillies, finely sliced
Bunch of spring onions (scallions), green tops only, finely shredded
2 Tbsp finely chopped fresh root ginger
A few sprigs of fresh coriander (cilantro)
1 lime, cut into wedges

Created especially for the Notting Hill Carnival, this sauce is FIRE and not for the faint-hearted. You've been warned!

When we got accepted to serve wings on the streets of the carnival, we knew we had to make a scene. In terms of footfall it is the highest capacity event we have ever been a part of. Serving wings among 3 million attendees, drinking rum and indulging in everything chicken – a perfect day out all in all.

We wanted to stand out from all the other vendors with their traditional jerk offerings, so we created the hottest carnival-inspired sauce ever and it is fair to say people did not forget it! Jamaican Heatwave is a creeper. The initial sweetness and delicious flavour from the Scotch bonnets make it so moreish that you're lulled into keeping going through the heat that follows. Be warned: if you do end up eating a whole portion of these bad boys, we recommend putting the toilet paper in the freezer the night before...

In a large bowl combine the wings with the dry spices and the buttermilk. Let marinate in the fridge for at least 1 hour or up to 4 hours. Combine the two flours and set aside. Drain the wings from the excess marinade and toss through the flour – keep chilled until ready to cook.

Add the sauce ingredients to a saucepan with 150ml (⅔ cup) water. Bring to the boil then reduce to a simmer until all the vegetables are cooked. Allow to cool slightly and blend with a stick blender.

Preheat a deep fryer to 180°C (350°F). Place the wings in the basket and lower slowly into the fryer. Cook for 7 or 8 minutes ensuring they hit 75°C (170°F) at the core of the thickest part of the wing and the juices run clear. If they don't hit 75°C (170°F) after the first 8 minutes just carry on cooking for a further minute.

This sauce is hot stuff... toss the wings with caution!!! Sprinkle over all the garnishes and get involved!

Maple-Candied Pecans
and Bacon

In a large bowl combine the wings with the dry spices and the buttermilk. Let marinate in the fridge for at least 1 hour or up to 4 hours. Combine the two flours and set aside. Drain the wings from the excess marinade and toss through the flour – keep chilled until ready to cook.

In a frying pan (skillet) toast the pecans until slightly golden and starting to brown around the edges. Once the nuts have browned, carefully add the 100ml maple syrup, ensuring all the nuts are evenly coated, and cook until the syrup has evaporated.

Pour the nuts onto a baking sheet lined with greased baking paper and allow to cool. Once cool, roughly chop and set aside.

Preheat the oven to 180°C (350°F) Gas 4.

Lay the bacon on a baking sheet and bake in the oven for about 15 minutes until turning golden. Remove from the oven, brush with the maple syrup and return to the oven for another 10 minutes until nicely glazed.

Preheat a deep fryer to 180°C (350°F). Place the wings in the basket and lower slowly into the fryer. Cook for 7 or 8 minutes ensuring they hit 75°C (170°F) at the core of the thickest part of the wing and the juices run clear. If they don't hit 75°C (170°F) after the first 8 minutes just carry on cooking for a further minute.

Arrange the wings on a serving dish and drizzle with extra maple syrup. Chop the glazed bacon into pieces and sprinkle on the top with the candied pecans. Garnish with spring onions, if using, then get ready to get sticky!

SERVES 4

1.25kg (2lb 12oz) chicken wings, tip removed, drums and flat separated
2 tsp celery salt
2 tsp white pepper
1 tsp black pepper
150ml (⅔ cup) buttermilk
250g (2½ cups) cornflour (cornstarch)
50g (⅓ cup) rice flour
6 rashers (slices) of bacon
50ml (¼ cup) maple syrup, plus extra to drizzle
2 or 3L (2 or 3qt) vegetable or rapeseed (canola) oil, for cooking
2 spring onions (scallions), finely chopped, to serve (optional)

CANDIED PECANS
50g (½ cup) pecans
100ml (scant ½ cup) maple syrup

Not just bacon but maple-candied bacon, to be precise; what's not to love? While the go-to sauce for wings is usually a hot one, maple-candied bacon with toasted pecans is an indulgent alternative for those with a sweeter tooth. The smokiness from the bacon, complemented by the sweetness of the caramelized maple syrup makes this a unique recipe for sticky-chicken-wing lovers. With the addition of toasted pecans, it makes the crunch factor Level 100.

Hoisin Buff Ting

Think about your favourite crispy aromatic dish from your local Chinese restaurant. That crispy meat served with hoisin sauce and wrapped in a pancake with spring onions and cucumber. Those textures and flavours which make it top of your list every time you order. Now turn that dish upside down and inside out with the addition of some chicken wings and that is exactly how we envisioned the Hoisin Buff Ting.

Crispy wings with a hoisin glaze, shredded crispy wontons and spring onion, served with a side of pickled cucumber.

In a large bowl combine the wings with the dry spices and the buttermilk. Let marinate in the fridge for at least 1 hour or up to 4 hours. Combine the two flours and set aside. Drain the wings from the excess marinade and toss through the flour – keep chilled until ready to cook.

Chop the garlic and ginger together to make a paste – you can use a mini blender for this or a pestle and mortar, if you prefer. Add the paste to a cold saucepan with the sesame oil and cook over a low heat until the garlic is cooked. Add the hoisin, sweet chilli, sugar, soy sauce, star anise, cinnamon and 100ml (scant ½ cup) water. Cook over a low heat until the sugar has dissolved and the sauce is thick enough to coat the back of a spoon.

Meanwhile, for the garnish, put the cucumber ribbons, vinegar, sugar and poppy seeds in a bowl, refrigerate and leave to pickle for about 20 minutes.

Preheat a deep fryer to 180°C (350°F). Place the wings in the basket and lower slowly into the fryer. Cook for 7 or 8 minutes ensuring they hit 75°C (170°F) at the core of the thickest part of the wing and the juices run clear. If they don't hit 75°C (170°F) after the first 8 minutes just carry on cooking for a further minute.

Toss the wings in the sticky glaze and stack them high on a plate. Arrange the spring onions on top with the crispy wontons, if using, and serve the cucumber alongside.

SERVES 4

1.25kg (2lb 12oz) chicken wings, tip removed, drums and flat separated
2 tsp celery salt
2 tsp white pepper
1 tsp black pepper
150ml (⅔ cup) buttermilk
250g (2½ cups) cornflour (cornstarch)
50g (⅓ cup) rice flour
2 or 3L (2 or 3qt) vegetable or rapeseed (canola) oil, for cooking

SAUCE
1 garlic clove
Hazelnut-sized piece of fresh root ginger, peeled
50ml (¼ cup) sesame oil
250g (1 cup) hoisin sauce
150g (¾ cup) sweet chilli sauce
3 Tbsp caster (granulated) sugar
1 Tbsp dark soy sauce
1 star anise
½ cinnamon stick

GARNISH
½ cucumber, cut into ribbons
1 Tbsp rice vinegar
1½ Tbsp caster (granulated) sugar
1 Tbsp poppy seeds
½ bunch of spring onions (scallions), green tops only, finely shredded
2 wonton wrappers, shredded and deep-fried (optional)

Szechuan Salt and Pepper

Less mess, no stress. Chicken wings are known for traditionally being smothered in sauce but the Szechuan bucks the trend by using only dry seasoning and garnish.

This recipe is for those who appreciate great flavour without the mess and sticky fingers. Crispy fried chicken seasoned with a five-spice Szechuan salt, green pepper, onions and curry leaf. Add a squeeze of lime to finish for a citrus fruity twist.

In a large bowl combine the wings with the dry spices and the buttermilk. Let marinate in the fridge for at least 1 hour or up to 4 hours. Combine the two flours and set aside. Drain the wings from the excess marinade and toss through the flour – keep chilled until ready to cook.

Preheat a deep fryer to 180°C (350°F). Place the wings in the basket and lower slowly into the fryer. Cook for 7 or 8 minutes ensuring they hit 75°C (170°F) at the core of the thickest part of the wing and the juices run clear. If they don't hit 75°C (170°F) after the first 8 minutes just carry on cooking for a further minute.

Heat some oil for the garnish in a wok and fry the chillies, spring onions, green pepper and curry leaves for a couple of minutes until crispy.

Pile the wings high on a plate, dust with the Szechuan seasoning and garnish with the fried chillies, spring onions, green pepper and curry leaves. Top with the coriander.

SERVES 4

1.25kg (2lb 12oz) chicken wings, tip removed, drums and flat separated
2 tsp celery salt
2 tsp white pepper
1 tsp black pepper
150ml (⅔ cup) buttermilk
250g (2½ cups) cornflour (cornstarch)
50g (⅓ cup) rice flour
2 or 3L (2 or 3qt) vegetable or rapeseed (canola) oil, for cooking
2 Tbsp Szechuan seasoning

GARNISH

Vegetable oil, for frying
2 fresh red chillies, finely sliced
Bunch of spring onions (scallions), green tops only, finely shredded
1 green (bell) pepper, deseeded and diced
A few curry leaves
A few sprigs of fresh coriander (cilantro) or cress

What Da Pho'

Inspired by Vietnamese ingredients and cooking techniques, the What Da Pho' has a unique taste due to its fish sauce base. While the sauce itself may not smell too appealing at first, when all the components are tossed together it is transformed into a delicious dish. We top it with toasted coconut, Thai basil, mint and fresh red chilli to add an extra element of heat.

In a large bowl combine the wings with the dry spices and the buttermilk. Let marinate in the fridge for at least 1 hour or up to 4 hours. Combine the two flours and set aside. Drain the wings from the excess marinade and toss through the flour – keep chilled until ready to cook.

For the sauce, in a saucepan bring 300ml (1¼ cups) water to the boil with the sugar and reduce until the mixture turns into a syrup. Add the fish sauce and continue to boil.

Combine the cornflour and enough water to create a paste – this will help thicken the sauce. Pour the cornflour mixture into the hot syrup and whisk in to ensure there are no lumps.

Preheat a deep fryer to 180°C (350°F). Place the wings in the basket and lower slowly into the fryer. Cook for 7 or 8 minutes ensuring they hit 75°C (170°F) at the core of the thickest part of the wing and the juices run clear. If they don't hit 75°C (170°F) after the first 8 minutes just carry on cooking for a further minute.

Grab a deep bowl and pile up the wings. Pour the sauce over the top, leaving a little puddle in the bottom. Top off with all the extra herbs, coconut, chillies, crispy onions and crushed peanuts. Serve with the lime wedges for squeezing over.

SERVES 4

1.25kg (2lb 12oz) chicken wings, tip removed, drums and flat separated
2 tsp celery salt
2 tsp white pepper
1 tsp black pepper
150ml (⅔ cup) buttermilk
250g (2½ cups) cornflour (cornstarch)
50g (⅓ cup) rice flour
2 or 3L (2 or 3qt) vegetable or rapeseed (canola) oil, for cooking
2 Tbsp Szechuan seasoning

SAUCE
200g (1 cup) caster (granulated) sugar
100ml (scant ½ cup) fish sauce
75g (¾ cup) cornflour (cornstarch)

GARNISH
½ bunch of fresh Thai basil, finely chopped
½ bunch of fresh mint, finely chopped
60g (¾ cup) desiccated (shredded) coconut, toasted
2 fresh red chillies, finely sliced
60g (1 cup) crispy onions
2 Tbsp crushed peanuts
1 lime, cut into wedges

Miso Caramel

SERVES 4

2 tsp celery salt
2 tsp white pepper
1 tsp black pepper
2 tsp smoked paprika
2 Tbsp vegetable oil
5 Tbsp miso paste
1.25kg (2lb 12oz) whole chicken wings
1 tsp sea salt
125g (scant ¾ cup) golden caster
   (granulated) sugar
50g (3½ Tbsp) butter
Freshly squeezed juice of 1 lime
1 Tbsp white sesame seeds, toasted

GARNISH
½ Granny Smith apple, sliced
2 Tbsp black sesame seeds, toasted

There's nothing like cooking on an open fire or BBQ to introduce extra flavour to your food and this recipe is one of those where it really benefits from this method of cooking. We came up with the recipe for a demonstration at Taste of London festival; 150 wings cooked over fire surrounded by great people with a real passion for good food – awesome.

If you don't have access to a fire pit or BBQ, don't worry: you can still achieve great results by baking this wing – it's about experimenting and giving it a try.

Preheat the oven to 200°C (400°F) Gas 6. Mix together the dry spices, oil, and 2 tablespoons of the miso paste. Pour over the chicken wings and toss to coat in the mixture. Lay the wings on a baking sheet in a single layer and season with sea salt before transferring to the preheated oven for 45 minutes. Alternatively, cook over an indirect heat on the BBQ (grill) for 25 minutes, or until the wing juices run clear.

In the meantime, add the sugar and 3 tablespoons of water to a small pan and heat over a very low heat until the sugar has dissolved.

Once dissolved and no longer grainy, turn the heat up to max to bring the mixture to the boil. Allow to boil and reduce for a few minutes until it takes on a nice amber caramel colour.

Remove the pan from the heat and immediately whisk in the butter, the remaining miso and the lime juice until the sauce is smooth and combined. Set the caramel aside until the chicken is done.

When the chicken is ready, take it out of the oven and pour the caramel over the wings, brushing it onto the chicken with a pastry brush. Sprinkle over the white sesame seeds and return to the oven for a further 5 minutes.

When ready, transfer to a serving plate, allow them to cool slightly, and serve garnished with the apple slices and black sesame seeds.

Grilled Wings with Stateside Sauce

For the sauce, add the mayonnaise to a bowl and pour in the cider vinegar. Stir in the lemon juice, Worcestershire sauce, grated horseradish, garlic granules and cracked black pepper.

Drizzle the wings with olive oil and season with the salt and peppers. Sprinkle over the dry spices and work them into the wings. Cook the wings over an indirect heat on the BBQ (grill) for 10–15 minutes. Char the lemon wedges.

Grab a pastry brush and coat the wings in the sauce and continue to cook for a further 10–15 minutes, basting every time they are turned over.

Serve with the blackened lemon wedges and extra sauce if needed.

SERVES 4

1.25kg (2lb 12oz) whole chicken wings
Olive oil
1 Tbsp sea salt
1 Tbsp white pepper
1 Tbsp black pepper
1 tsp smoked paprika
1 tsp dried oregano
1 tsp dried chilli (red pepper) flakes
1 tsp cayenne pepper
Lemon wedges, to serve

STATESIDE SAUCE
150ml (¾ cup) full-fat mayonnaise
150ml (⅔ cup) cider vinegar
Freshly squeezed juice of 1 lemon
3 Tbsp Worcestershire sauce
Freshly grated horseradish, to taste
1 Tbsp garlic granules
2 tsp cracked black pepper

There are so many versions of this wing but one part always remains the same: mayonnaise! OK, hot mayonnaise used as a glaze sounds kind of weird but don't knock it until you've tried it. This wing is at its best on a BBQ, kissed by red-hot flames.

Be generous with dressing and you will thank us for it later.

Jerk' It

Get the BBQ on and crack open a couple of ice-cold brews before getting your jerk on. The best way to cook jerk chicken is by grilling or smoking it. Trust us, we have tried every way. If there is not a smokey char to the chicken, it is just not jerk. Unfortunately, we are plagued by rainy skies and short summers in the UK, so we have included recipes for indoor and outdoor cooking. That way, you can jerk off all year round.

The other key to this recipe is in how you glaze and baste the chicken while it is being cooked. It requires a high flame and a Jamaican beer to glaze it.

The wings are accompanied by charred citrus, cooked alongside the chicken, to give it that authentic flavour.

Preheat the oven to 200°C (400°F) Gas 6 or fire up the BBQ.

In a blender, blitz the spring onions, thyme, Scotch bonnet, dry spices and sugar. Apply the seasoning over the wings, cover and refrigerate for a couple of hours or more to allow the flavour to develop.

Transfer the chicken to a baking sheet and bake for 15 minutes. After the first 15 minutes, remove the wings and baste with the lager. Return to the oven to finish cooking for a further 10–15 minutes. Alternatively, cook on the BBQ (grill) over a medium heat, turning and basting with the lager until deeply coloured and the chicken juices run clear – about 30 minutes.

Grill the lemons, cut sides down, on a very hot griddle pan until charred.

Serve the wings with the charred lemons and the coriander sprinkled over.

SERVES 4

2 spring onions (scallions), roughly chopped
1 sprig of thyme
1 fresh red Scotch bonnet, stems removed (wear gloves, these are seriously hot!) and roughly chopped
1 Tbsp garlic granules
1 Tbsp ground cinnamon
1 Tbsp ground allspice
1 Tbsp smoked paprika
1 Tbsp ground nutmeg
1 Tbsp cayenne pepper
1 Tbsp dried parsley
1 Tbsp white pepper
1 Tbsp ground cumin
2 tsp sea salt
1 tsp ground cloves
1 tsp brown sugar
1.25kg (2lb 12oz) chicken wings, tip removed, drums and flat separated
220ml (1 cup) Red Stripe lager

GARNISH
2 lemons, halved
½ bunch of fresh coriander (cilantro)

Satays' faction Guaranteed

SERVES 4

1.25kg (2lb 12oz) chicken wings, tip
   removed, drums and flat separated
2 tsp celery salt
2 tsp white pepper
1 tsp black pepper
1 tsp Chinese five spice
2 or 3L (2 or 3qt) vegetable or rapeseed
   (canola) oil, for cooking, optional

SATAY SAUCE

Hazelnut-sized piece of fresh root
   ginger, peeled
½ fresh lemongrass stalk
2 Tbsp vegetable oil
200ml (scant 1 cup) coconut milk
100ml (scant ½ cup) sweet chilli sauce
50ml (¼ cup) dark soy sauce
250g (1 cup) crunchy peanut butter
2 tsp madras powder
Salt and black pepper

GARNISH

1 tsp dried chilli (red pepper) flakes
1 tsp black sesame seeds
75g (scant ¾ cup) roasted peanuts,
   chopped
2 spring onions (scallions), green tops
   only, finely shredded
A few sprigs of fresh coriander
   (cilantro), chopped
½ cucumber, cut into sticks

Nuts about nuts or a peanut butter fanatic? This one is for you! Whether your preference is smooth or crunchy, this recipe is a peanut butter lover's dream. Marinated chicken, cooked on a grill and flame-kissed while being brushed down with homemade satay sauce – unbeatable.

Add some cucumber, spring onion and coriander for those finishing touches to tone down the richness and it's satays'faction guaranteed.

In a large bowl combine the wings with the dry spices. Let marinate in the fridge for at least 1 hour or up to 4 hours – keep chilled until ready to cook.

Chop the ginger into a paste with the lemongrass. Add the paste to a small pan with the oil and heat over a low heat until soft. Add the coconut milk, sweet chilli and soy sauces, then bring to the boil. Remove the pan from the heat and whisk in the peanut butter and madras powder. Season with a little salt and pepper if needed.

Cook the marinated wings on a BBQ (grill) for 10–15 minutes, allowing them to char around the edges. Baste the wings with the satay sauce, reserving some to serve, and continue to cook for a further 10 minutes, turning the wings after each baste.

Alternatively, preheat a deep fryer to 180°C (350°F). Place the wings in the basket and lower slowly into the fryer. Cook for 7 or 8 minutes ensuring they hit 75°C (170°F) at the core of the thickest part of the wing and the juices run clear. If they don't hit 75°C (170°F) after the first 8 minutes just carry on cooking for a further minute. Toss the wings in the sauce, reserving some to serve.

Serve the wings sprinkled with the chilli flakes, sesame seeds, chopped peanuts, spring onions and coriander. Spoon the extra satay sauce into a small bowl for dipping and finish with the cucumber on the side.

Roasted Bone Marrow
BBQ Wings

In a large bowl combine the wings with the dry spices and let marinate in the fridge for at least 1 hour or up to 4 hours – keep chilled until ready to cook.

Preheat the oven to 170°C (325°F) Gas 3. For the marrow bones, place the bones in a deep ovenproof dish and roast for 30–40 minutes until all the marrow has melted. Pour off the liquid gold and discard the bones.

In a saucepan bring the vinegar to the boil and reduce by two thirds. Add the sugar and paprika and whisk until smooth. Pour in the ketchup, bone marrow liquid and the cola, and continue to reduce until combined and glossy. At this point add the Worcestershire sauce and the Bourbon – add a little extra if you're feeling it.

Transfer the marinated wings into an ovenproof dish and pour the sauce over the top. Cover the dish with foil and bake in the oven for 30 minutes, giving them a shake every now and again.

Remove the foil from the wings and continue to cook for a further 15–20 minutes, making sure you baste them every 5 minutes with the sauce.

The wings are ready when they start to look sticky and the core temperature Is 75°C (170°F) or over.

Serve these wings in the same container you cooked them in – they will fall off the bone and won't be around for long. Keep the extra Bourbon close at hand, too!

SERVES 4

1.25kg (2lb 12oz) chicken wings, tip removed, drums and flat separated
2 tsp celery salt
2 tsp white pepper
1 tsp black pepper
1 tsp smoked paprika
1 tsp garlic granules
1 tsp onion powder

WINGMANS BBQ SAUCE
2kg (4lb 8oz) beef marrow bones
500ml (2 cups) red wine vinegar
150g (¾ cup) soft dark brown sugar
5 Tbsp smoked paprika
500ml (2 cups) tomato ketchup
150ml (⅔ cup) cola
A dash of Worcestershire sauce
150ml (⅔ cup) Bourbon whiskey

NOTE
If you purchase the marrow bones from your butcher you can ask them to cut them down to a smaller size.

Traditional BBQ sauce has no heat to it but is sweet, sticky, smokey and downright delicious. BUT, we can assure you that our roasted bone marrow version takes the sauce to a whole new level: think sweet and smokey BBQ sauce on steroids – it's the only way to do it justice.

You should be able to get bone marrow from your local butcher. It's well priced and filled with flavour and our Number One go-to for making the most flavoursome BBQ sauce around.

Finally, we recommend a touch of Bourbon for even more smokiness (as well as an excuse for a cheeky tipple).

The Honey Monster

SERVES 4

1.25kg (2lb 12oz) chicken wings, tip
  removed, drums and flat separated
2 tsp celery salt
2 tsp ground white pepper
1 tsp freshly ground black pepper
2 tsp garlic granules
2 tsp salt

SAUCE
200g (1 cup) golden caster (granulated)
  sugar
100g (6 Tbsp) honey
Zest of 2½ lemons
Large piece of fresh root ginger, peeled
  and thinly sliced
2 large shallots, finely chopped
75g (5 Tbsp) butter
Black pepper, to taste

This recipe it so simple to prepare that Ben's mum swears by it. It's sweet and sticky, with just enough lemon to keep it fresh and zingy.

The secret to this is the pepper. Don't be tempted to use storebought ground black pepper – fresh is best and all the hard work and elbow grease needed to grind it will result in such tasty wings that you'll be licking your lips and going back in for another and another...

In a large bowl combine the wings with the dry spices and let marinate in the fridge for at least 1 hour or up to 4 hours – keep chilled until ready to cook.

Preheat the oven to 180°C (350°F) Gas 4.

In a small saucepan bring 150ml (⅔ cup) water to the boil with the sugar. Add the honey, zest of 2 lemons and the ginger to the syrup. Allow to reduce slightly until the syrup takes on both flavours. Sieve the syrup into a clean container.

Soften the shallots in a small pan with the butter. Pour the syrup onto the softened shallots and mix together.

Line up the wings on a wire rack over a baking sheet and bake for 15 minutes.

After 15 minutes, brush the wings with the glaze and continue to cook, applying fresh glaze every 5 minutes for a further 15 minutes. Reserve some glaze to serve.

Put the wings in a bowl and toss with a little reserved glaze ensuring they are fully coated. Arrange in a serving dish and garnish with the remaining lemon zest and 5–10 twists of black pepper.

Cajun Persuasion

A crucial process in making the most flavoursome wings and which often gets neglected is the dry rub. Even if it is a simple salt and pepper mix, it is the additional penetration of flavour into the meat that takes the taste from zero to hero. The Cajun Persuasion uses a spiced rub which is left to flavour the meat for a minimum of 24 hours.

Once cooked, serve them with pickled red chillies and coriander yogurt dipping sauce on the side – it's a magical flavour combo.

In a large bowl combine the wings with the Cajun seasoning and the oil. Leave to marinate overnight.

In a small pan bring the vinegar to the boil with the sugar and reduce by a third. Add a splash of water if the pickle liquid is too sweet. Pour over the chillies and leave to sit in the fridge overnight – this can be done a few days in advance.

For the coriander yogurt, remove the coriander leaves from the stalks and blend in a mini food processor with the natural yogurt and sour cream. Season to taste.

Preheat the oven to 180°C (350°F) Gas 4. Place the onion slices on a baking sheet. Pour over the marinated wings and mix through with the onions. Bake in the oven for 25–30 minutes until the wings take on a deep golden colour. Make sure you shake the baking sheet and turn the wings over every 10 minutes.

Pile up the wings and spoon over the excess sauce and soft onions from the baking sheet. Spoon over some of the coriander yogurt and serve with the pickled chillies, lime wedges and coriander sprigs.

SERVES 4

1.25kg (2lb 12oz) whole chicken wings
5 Tbsp blackened Cajun seasoning
3 Tbsp vegetable oil
1 large white onion, sliced
2 limes, cut into wedges, to serve

PICKLED CHILLIES
200ml (scant 1 cup) rice wine vinegar
300g (1½ cups) caster (granulated) sugar
500g (1lb 2oz) fresh red chillies, sliced

CORIANDER YOGURT
½ bunch of fresh coriander (cilantro), plus extra to serve
100ml (½ cup) natural (plain) yogurt
50g (3 Tbsp) sour cream
Salt and black pepper, to taste

Grilled or fried, stuffed in a roll or between two slices of bread... Whether you call it a burger, a sandwich or a fried chicken bun is irrelevant. What is important is that it needs to be full of flavour, piled high and deeply satisfying – bite after bite. There are no fixed rules here.

Be bold, season generously and get involved.

THE ROUTE 66

SERVES 4

100g (¾ cup) plain (all-purpose) flour
1 tsp garlic granules
1 tsp onion powder
1 tsp dried oregano
2 tsp celery salt
2 tsp white pepper
2 eggs
250g (6 cups) panko breadcrumbs
3 tsp salt
1 tsp black pepper
4 skinless, boneless chicken thighs
2 or 3L (2 or 3qt) vegetable or rapeseed (canola) oil, for cooking

GARNISH

50ml (¼ cup) red wine vinegar
2 Tbsp caster (granulated) sugar
1 red onion, sliced
100g (1 cup) Bread and Butter Pickles (see page 184), or storebought, sliced

TO SERVE

4 sesame brioche buns, halved
50g (3½ Tbsp) butter, melted
125g (scant ½ cup) Burnt Onion Jam (see page 183)
1 baby gem lettuce, leaves separated
150ml (⅔ cup) Buttermilk Ranch dressing (see page 183)
4 slices American cheese, such as Monterey Jack

49

FUN WITH BUNS

Now, not all superheroes wear capes but all the boldest American-style chicken burgers wear these base ingredients: chicken, cheese, mayo and lettuce. With so few components, you may wonder what factors determine the best-tasting chicken burger, but it is simply down to the highest-quality ingredients.

The Route 66 is our take on the classic American chicken sandwich, using panko-breaded chicken thigh, gem lettuce, Monterey Jack cheese and pickles.

Set up 3 separate bowls. In the first, combine the flour with all of the dry spices and seasoning. Crack the eggs into the second bowl and whisk until smooth. In the third bowl, add the panko breadcrumbs, salt and black pepper.

Trim the chicken thighs removing excess fat and any gristle from the meat. Pass the thighs through the flour, eggs and the breadcrumbs. Set aside on a plate until needed – don't do this too far in advance as the breadcrumbs will absorb the moisture in the chicken and the crust will not be as crumbly as required.

Add the red wine vinegar and sugar to the sliced red onions and set aside until soft and deep purple in colour.

Preheat a deep fryer to 170°C (340°F). Place the breaded thighs in the basket and lower slowly into the fryer. Cook for 8 minutes ensuring they hit 75°C (170°F) at the core of the thickest part of the thigh. If they don't hit 75°C (170°F) after the first 8 minutes, continue cooking for a further minute.

To build the burger, toast the sliced buns in a dry frying pan (skillet) until lightly coloured. Brush with the melted butter and return to the pan until a deep golden colour. Add the onion jam to the bottom bun then add the lettuce. On the top bun spoon on the ranch dressing, being generous. As soon as the chicken thigh is cooked and golden, add a slice of American cheese and place on top of the lettuce. Garnish with the pickled onions and the pickles. Top with the other half of the bun and give the whole thing a little squeeze. Best served with ice cold beer and a couple of mates.

NOTORIOUS P.I.G.

For the pulled pork, preheat the oven to 140°C (275°F) Gas 1. In a small bowl, combine the brown sugar, salt, paprika, garlic granules, onion powder and black pepper. Rub all over the pork shoulder.

In a large pan sear the pork on all sides until nicely coloured. Place the pork shoulder in a deep ovenproof dish and pour over the apple juice, add the garlic and cover with a lid. Transfer to the oven and cook low and slow until the pork is beginning to tenderize, about 2½ hours. Remove the lid and cook until the pork is very tender and pulls apart easily with a fork. Add the BBQ sauce and season if needed.

For the bacon butter, render the fat out of the pancetta lardons in a dry frying pan over a medium heat. Once the pancetta is golden, add the butter and a splash of water. Strain through a sieve and keep warm until the burger is being built.

For the pickled cabbage, bring the vinegar to the boil with a splash of water, the sugar and the caraway seeds. Pour over the shredded white cabbage and allow to cool in the vinegar.

Prepare the chicken thighs. In a large bowl combine the flour, dry spices and the baking powder and in a second bowl pour in the buttermilk. Trim the thighs to remove any excess skin, fat and gristle.

Pass the thighs through the seasoned flour into the buttermilk and then back through the flour. Preheat a deep fryer to 180°C (350°F). Slowly lower the prepared thighs into the hot oil and cook for about 10 minutes until golden brown and thoroughly cooked, ensuring they hit 75°C (170°F) at the core of the thickest part of the thigh and the juices run clear.

Reheat the pulled pork until piping hot. Grill the buns on a griddle and brush with the bacon butter. Add the pickled cabbage and crispy chicken. Pile on the pulled pork. Crush the bacon crisps on top and add a huge dollop of chorizo jam. Throw on the lid and take a bite!

SERVES 4

4 skinless, boneless chicken thighs
100g (¾ cup) plain (all-purpose) flour
1 tsp garlic granules
1 tsp onion powder
1 tsp dried oregano
2 tsp cayenne pepper
2 tsp celery salt
3 tsp salt
2 tsp white pepper
1 tsp black pepper
2 tsp baking powder
300ml (1¼ cups) buttermilk
2 or 3L (2 or 3qt) vegetable or rapeseed (canola) oil, for cooking

PULLED PORK
3 Tbsp brown sugar
1 tsp salt
1 Tbsp smoked paprika
1 Tbsp garlic granules
1 Tbsp onion powder
1 Tbsp black pepper
1kg (2lb 4oz) boneless pork shoulder
300ml (1¼ cups) apple juice
1 head of garlic
250ml (1 cup) Wingmans BBQ Sauce (see page 40)

BACON BUTTER
100g (scant ¾ cup) smoked pancetta lardons
50g (3½ Tbsp) butter

PICKLED CABBAGE
150ml (⅔ cup) cider vinegar
90g (½ cup) caster (granulated) sugar
1 tsp caraway seeds
200g (7oz) white cabbage, shredded

Even Biggie would
have of approved this.
It's pure gluttony:
buttermilk-fried thigh,
pulled pork, chorizo
jam and pickled
cabbage served on
a toasted bun and
smothered in bacon
butter. If you can't
decide between a
beef burger, a chicken
burger or a pulled pork
bun, then give this one
a shot. A monster eat...

TO SERVE
4 sesame brioche buns,
 halved
1 packet bacon-flavoured
 crisps (chips), such as
 Frazzles
Chorizo Jam (see page 185)

CRUMPLESTILTSKIN

Toasted crumpets (yes, that's right, crumpets, or English muffins if you're in the US of A!) + buttermilk chicken breast + Stilton butter + fig and bacon jam + crispy chicken skin = the one and only Crumplestiltskin.

Now, we don't judge, so if the crumpets justify this as a breakfast burger then be our guest...we may even join you.

Preheat the oven to 180°C (350°F) Gas 4. Remove the chicken skin from the breasts and stretch out on a baking sheet lined with baking paper. Season with salt and pepper and cook in the oven for about 10 minutes until golden and crisp. Retain for garnishing.

Work the Stilton into the butter and mix in the Dijon mustard. Set to one side.

For the candied bacon, lay the bacon out on a baking sheet and cook in the oven until starting to colour. Brush with the maple syrup and return to the oven until fully cooked and charred around the edges. Set to one side.

In a large bowl, combine the flour, dry spices and the baking powder and in a second bowl pour in the buttermilk.

Lay the breasts between two pieces of clingfilm (plastic wrap) and flatten to 2cm (¾in) thick using a rolling pin.

Preheat a deep fryer to 180°C (350°F). Pass the flattened breast through the seasoned flour into the buttermilk and then back through the flour. Slowly lower the breast into the hot oil and cook for about 15 minutes until golden brown and thoroughly cooked, ensuring they hit 75°C (170°F) at the core of the thickest part of the breast and the juices run clear.

Toast the crumpets and smear the Stilton butter over the crumpets making sure it fills all the holes. For each serving, add fig and bacon jam to two crumpets. Place a crispy chicken piece on the bottom crumpet and top with the crispy skin and two rashers of candied bacon. Finish off with the top crumpet and a little extra Stilton if you have it to spare.

SERVES 4

4 small chicken breast fillets, skin on
100g (¾ cup) plain (all-purpose) flour
1 tsp garlic granules
1 tsp onion powder
1 tsp dried oregano
2 tsp cayenne pepper
2 tsp celery salt
3 tsp salt
2 tsp white pepper
1 tsp black pepper
2 tsp baking powder
300ml (1¼ cups) buttermilk
2 or 3L (2 or 3qt) vegetable or rapeseed (canola) oil, for cooking
8 thick crumpets (English muffins)
Fig and Bacon Jam (see page 184), to serve

STILTON BUTTER
100g (3½oz) Stilton cheese
50g (3½ Tbsp) butter, softened
1 tsp Dijon mustard

CANDIED BACON
8 rashers (slices) of smoked streaky bacon
150ml (⅔ cup) maple syrup

BEIJING
BLOCK PARTY

An Asian twist on an American classic and no fryer necessary – sesame-glazed grilled chicken breast, Shanghai mayo, crispy Asian slaw, roasted peanut and chilli powder. Perfect.

Shred all the slaw vegetables and coriander into long, thin strips. Mix the vinegar with the sugar and sesame oil until the sugar has dissolved. Pour over the slaw, add a pinch of salt and allow to sit and soften slightly.

Stir the Shanghai sauce into the mayo and keep chilled.

Preheat a griddle pan over a high heat. Butterfly the chicken breasts and brush with oil. Heavily season with salt and pepper. Add the chicken to the griddle pan. Once the chicken has changed colour around the edges flip over and brush with some of the sesame dressing. Continue to brush with the dressing and turn until fully cooked and golden, and the core temperature is 75°C (170°F).

Toast the buns and spoon a little of the Shanghai mayo on the bottom half. Add a lettuce leaf and the grilled chicken. Top with the slaw and add more sesame dressing. Sprinkle over the crushed peanuts, coriander and togarashi.

SERVES 4

4 skinless, boneless chicken breasts
Oil, for brushing
125ml (½ cup) Roasted Sesame Dressing (see page 174)
Salt and black pepper

ASIAN SLAW
1 cucumber
200g (7oz) daikon
1 large carrot
2 spring onions (scallions)
30g (1 cup) fresh coriander (cilantro) leaves
100ml (scant ½ cup) rice wine vinegar
50g (¼ cup) caster (granulated) sugar
2 tsp sesame oil

SHANGHAI MAYO
50ml (¼ cup) Shanghai Sauce (see page 174)
150ml (¾ cup) Japanese mayonnaise

GARNISH
4 seeded brioche buns, halved
1 baby gem lettuce, leaves separated
100g (1 cup) crushed roasted peanuts
A few sprigs of fresh coriander (cilantro), chopped
4 tsp togarashi spice blend

SEOUL SISTA SLIDERS

Set up three bowls: flour in the first with all the garlic granules, onion powder and celery salt, 2½ teaspoons of the sea salt and both the peppers; beaten eggs in the second bowl; and panko in the third with the remaining salt and dried oregano.

Coat the thigh halves in the flour, then egg, then breadcrumbs, making sure to press the crumbs into the chicken. Keep chilled until ready to cook.

Slice the pineapple quarters into 5mm (¼in) slices. Heat a griddle pan and add the pineapple, allowing it to colour and char slightly before removing and setting to one side.

For the butter, squeeze the kimchi in a clean J-cloth to remove any excess moisture. Blend in a food processor until smooth. Work the kimchi into the softened butter and keep at room temperature until needed.

With a speed peeler, make thin ribbons of the cucumber and place in a bowl. Mix the ponzu, black sesame seeds, coriander, sugar and sesame oil and adjust the seasoning if needed with a touch of salt – if you like your pickle sweeter, add a touch more sugar. Set to one side.

Preheat a deep fryer to 180°C (350°F). Slowly lower the prepared thighs into the hot oil and cook for 7 or 8 minutes ensuring they hit 75°C (170°F) at the core of the thickest part of the thigh. Fry until golden brown.

To build the sliders, toast the brioche buns and brush with the kimchi butter. Warm the Seoulja Boi sauce in a saucepan. Top the base bun with roasted sesame dressing and add lettuce. Dip the cooked chicken in the warmed Seoulja Boi sauce to completely coat it then place on top of the lettuce. Add grilled pineapple and ribbons of ponzu cucumber (make sure you get the coriander and sesame seeds in there, too). Finish off with the spring onions, a drizzle of the sesame dressing and the toasted top bun.

SERVES 4

200g (1½ cups) plain (all-purpose) flour
2 tsp garlic granules
2 tsp onion powder
3 tsp celery salt
5 tsp sea salt
4 tsp white pepper
2 tsp black pepper
3 eggs, beaten
350g (8 cups) panko breadcrumbs
2 tsp dried oregano
6 skinless, boneless chicken thighs, trimmed of excess fat and gristle and halved
2 or 3L (2 or 3qt) vegetable or rapeseed (canola) oil, for cooking
12 brioche slider buns, halved, to serve

KIMCHI BUTTER
100g (1 cup) kimchi
150g (½ cup plus 2 Tbsp) butter, softened

PONZU CUCUMBERS
1 cucumber
150ml (⅔ cup) ponzu
2 tsp black sesame seeds
20g (scant 1 cup) fresh coriander (cilantro), chopped
75g (⅓ cup) caster (granulated) sugar
2 tsp sesame oil

GARNISH
1 pineapple, peeled, cored and
   quartered
300ml (1¼ cups) Seoulja Boi Sauce
   (see page 18)
100ml (⅓ cup) Roasted Sesame
   Dressing (see page 174)
1 iceberg lettuce, shredded
Bunch of spring onions (scallions),
   green tops only, sliced diagonally

Our good pal DJ BBQ (Christian Stevenson),
legend of his name, lord of fire and all round
pretty decent dude, approached us to feature in
his most recent burger bible. We were honoured
to say the least and knew that we had to produce
something epic in line with his sensational
culinary creations.

Using our award-winning Seoulja Boi Sauce, the
Seoul Sista Sliders were born. Sliders are meant
to be for sharing but we guarantee you will not
want to share these!

SHARING'S

CARING

Let's be honest, when it comes to food, no one likes to share, but all good things come to those who do!

In fact, a recent study has shown that 15% of friendships are lost over food jealousy. We hope with the following recipes we can help contribute to boosting this statistic.

Whether it's a starter or side, those little dishes floating around the table are always the most memorable – whether you have actually been kind enough to share them or not!

SWEET AND STICKY

BUFFALO NUTS

SERVES 4

100g (¾ cup) cashew nuts
150g (1 cup) blanched almonds
100g (¾ cup) blanched hazelnuts
150g (1⅓ cups) pecans
250g (1¼ cups) caster (granulated)
    sugar
150ml (¾ cup) Buffalo Sauce
    (see page 175)

Buffalo nuts unite! These sweet and spicy nuts will have you going back again and again. They're great as a treat or with a pitcher of beer – either way, they're a sure-fire crowd pleaser.

Preheat the oven to 150°C (300°F) Gas 2. Toast all of the nuts together in a dry frying pan (skillet) until slightly charred and golden.

Add the sugar to a heavy-based saucepan. Add 50ml (¼ cup) water so the sugar turns to a wet sandy texture. Place on a medium–high heat and bring to the boil. As the sugar syrup boils, brush the inside of the saucepan with a wet brush to remove any formed sugar crystals.

Once the sugar has taken on a deep caramel colour, remove from the heat and pour in half of the buffalo sauce, taking extra care as the caramel will bubble and could spit. Swirl the pan to combine the sauces, then add the rest of the sauce, stir, and pour it over the nuts to coat them completely.

Once the nuts are fully coated, pour onto a baking sheet and cook in the oven for 15 minutes. Allow to cool and then break into little buffalo clusters.

BOURBON-GLAZED

BACON JERKY

This one hardly needs an explanation. Bourbon + bacon + jerky. Enough said.

Light the coals on the BBQ (grill). Allow the coals to catch fire and burn off until all the black smoke has stopped, the coals are coated in grey ash and glowing amber. Arrange the majority of the coals to one side of the BBQ creating a high temperature cook zone and a cooler one.

Add the sugar, syrup and bourbon to a small saucepan and heat on the edge of the grill until the sugar has dissolved.

Place the bacon over the hot side of the grill rack and cook until golden on one side. Once golden, flip the bacon and brush the golden side with the glaze.

Repeat the process over the cooler side of the grill until the bacon is crispy, sticky and a deep brown colour, then remove and leave to cool.

These are best eaten straightaway or while slightly warm, and it's even worth cooking another batch because, let's be honest, there's just never enough bacon!

MAKES 12 PIECES

100g (½ cup) soft dark brown sugar
50ml (¼ cup) maple syrup
25ml (5 tsp) Buffalo Trace (Bourbon whiskey)
12 rashers (slices) of good-quality, thick-cut smoked bacon

Oh yessssssss – a quick and easy recipe for crispy chicken greatness. Heavenly is an understatement.

CRISPY CHICKEN SKIN WITH

ROSEMARY SALT AND SUMAC

MAKES 12 PIECES

12 pieces of chicken skin, ideally from
    the breast meat
A few pinches of sumac
Zest of 1 lemon

ROSEMARY SALT
1 Tbsp fresh rosemary leaves
25g (1oz) dried rosemary
100g (½ cup) sea salt

For the rosemary salt, preheat a deep fryer to 180°C (350°F). Deep-fry the fresh rosemary until they look like the moisture has gone and they're crisp. Carefully remove from the oil and drain well. Add to a food processor with the dried rosemary and sea salt and blitz.

Preheat the oven to 180°C (350°F) Gas 4.

Stretch the chicken skin out and divide between 2 or 3 baking sheets, ensuring that the skins don't touch. Sprinkle with 1 tablespoon of rosemary salt, the sumac and lemon zest.

Cook for 10 minutes or until golden and crisp. Carefully remove from the baking sheet and allow to cool slightly before tucking in!

BUFFALO CHICKEN DIP

WITH FRICKLES AND RANCH

If a recipe ever existed for the best way to use up leftover roast chicken, this would be it! This is a crowd pleaser, time and time again. If you're a buffalo sauce fan but don't like all the tang, then this one is also for you. The ranch and cheeses in the recipe mellow out the vinegar and result in a creamy, moreish dip that you won't be able to control yourself with!

If you're making this for friends, be sure to organize crowd control beforehand.

Preheat the oven to 170°C (325°F) Gas 3.

Heat the cream cheese, ranch dressing, buffalo sauce, pepper to taste, and garlic granules in a small pan over a medium–low heat. Whisk constantly until combined and creamy. Remove from the heat.

Stir in the spring onions, chives, shredded chicken, a pinch of salt and two-thirds of the Cheddar and mozzarella.

Transfer the mixture to an ovenproof dish and sprinkle with the remaining grated cheeses. Bake for about 20 minutes, or until golden and bubbly.

For the frickles, combine both flours with the dried seasonings and baking powder in one bowl and put the buttermilk in another bowl. Roll the gherkin slices in the seasoned flour, pass through the buttermilk and then back through the flour mix.

Preheat a deep fryer to 180°C (350°F). Deep-fry the gherkins until crisp and golden – sprinkle with sea salt when cooked.

Serve the frickles alongside the chicken dip. Pop the carrot and celery in a bowl and serve with more ranch dressing and a selection of bits to dip.

SERVES 8

2 x 250g (8oz) tubs of cream cheese
150ml (¾ cup) Buttermilk Ranch dressing (see page 183), plus extra to serve
150ml (¾ cup) Buffalo Sauce (see page 175)
2 tsp garlic granules
3 spring onions (scallions), sliced
Small bunch of fresh chives, chopped
750g (1lb 10oz) cooked shredded chicken
100g (1 generous cup) grated Cheddar cheese
75g (⅔ cup) grated mozzarella
Salt and black pepper

FRICKLES
300g (2¼ cups) plain (all-purpose) flour
150g (1¼ cups) cornflour (cornstarch)
2 Tbsp garlic granules
2 Tbsp onion powder
1 Tbsp sea salt
1 Tbsp black pepper
1 tsp baking powder
200ml (¾ cup) buttermilk
4 whole large gherkins, sliced in half lengthways
2 or 3L (2 or 3qt) vegetable or rapeseed (canola) oil, for cooking

TO SERVE
Carrot sticks
Celery sticks
Selection of bagel or pretzel thins, tortilla chips, ciabatta croutons

CORNBREAD WITH BONE MARROW
AND HONEY BUTTER

No one in the world loves cornbread as much as Ben does, which is why he has perfected this extraordinary bone marrow and honey butter version. He loves cornbread more than peanut butter loves jelly and if you're looking for a sharer to make people love you just as much, then look no further.

For the bone marrow and honey butter, roughly cut the bone marrow into small rounds. Place in a small saucepan over a low heat ensuring it only melts and does not boil.

Once fully melted, increase the heat and add the honey, then season to taste. At this point it is important to bring to the boil once and then immediately remove the pan from the heat. Whisk in the butter and continue whisking until the mixture has cooled and the butter has emulsified.

Preheat the oven to 200°C (400°F) Gas 6.

For the cornbread, in a large bowl mix together the flour, cornmeal, sugar, baking powder and a pinch of salt. In a second bowl, mix together the egg, milk and oil. Combine the two mixtures and beat together ensuring there are no lumps. Pour into a shallow baking pan and bake until the cornbread has risen slightly – about 10–12 minutes or until a skewer inserted in the middle comes out clean. Turn out and allow to cool on a wire rack before cutting into soldiers or squares.

Pile the cornbread onto a board and spoon the cooled butter into a small serving dish. Be quick with this as it won't last long!

SERVES 4

125g (¾ cup) plain (all-purpose) flour
125g (scant 1 cup) cornmeal (polenta)
135g (⅔ cup) caster (granulated) sugar
3 tsp baking powder
1 egg
240ml (1 cup) whole milk
80ml (⅓ cup) vegetable oil
Salt and black pepper

BONE MARROW
AND HONEY BUTTER
100g (3½oz) bone marrow melt
50g (3 Tbsp) honey
150g (½ cup plus 2 Tbsp) butter, cubed

ROASTED GARLIC AND MISO-GLAZED CHICKEN

THIGHS WITH CARAMELIZED WALNUTS

SERVES 4

1 head of garlic
Light olive oil, for baking and frying
200g (⅔ cup) white miso paste
100ml (scant ½ cup) mirin
50ml (¼ cup) light soy sauce
150g (¾ cup) caster (granulated) sugar
8 skinless, boneless chicken thighs
1 sheet nori seaweed, cut into strips,
  to serve
Salt and black pepper

CARAMELIZED WALNUTS
150g (¾ cup) caster (granulated) sugar
50g (⅓ cup) walnut halves

As a starter or side, miso thinks you need to try these!

Preheat the oven to 170°C (325°F) Gas 3. Cut the top off the head of garlic, drizzle with oil and sprinkle with a little salt and pepper. Wrap in foil and bake slowly for 45 minutes to an hour, until the garlic takes on a deep brown colour – doing this will mellow out the garlic and completely change the flavour.

Combine the miso, mirin, soy sauce, sugar and half of the roasted garlic (squeeze the roasted cloves out of their skins) in a small saucepan and heat until the sugar has dissolved and all the ingredients have come together.

For the walnuts, heat the sugar with a small splash of water and allow to caramelize. Once your sugar has turned a deep caramel colour, add the walnuts and coat in the sugar. Pour the caramelized walnuts onto a greased sheet of baking paper and leave to cool.

Preheat a griddle pan to medium high until the pan starts to smoke slightly. Drizzle a little oil over the chicken thighs and sprinkle with a little salt and pepper. Add to the pan and colour on the first side. Turn the thighs over and brush with the miso glaze. Reduce the heat of the pan at this point, making sure the glaze does not catch and burn. Repeat the process until the thighs are cooked and super sticky.

Plate up and sprinkle with the walnuts and nori, with the extra roasted garlic on the side.

NOTE
The chicken for this recipe is best cooked on an open fire over a BBQ; however, it can be adapted to cook indoors, as described here.

Comfort food comes in all shapes and sizes but what remains the same is it needs to stick to your bones, warm you up and make you smile! This recipe is that for us. Creamy celeriac, sticky chicken and bourbon-glazed onions – say no more.

STICKY BBQ CHICKEN THIGHS WITH

CELERIAC AND BOURBON-GLAZED ONIONS

SERVES 4

8 skinless, boneless chicken thighs
200ml (¾ cup) Wingmans BBQ Sauce
   (see page 40)
Salt

CELERIAC
1 celeriac
300ml (1¼ cups) milk
150g (½ cup plus 2 Tbsp) butter
300ml (1¼ cups) chicken stock
A few sprigs of fresh thyme
1 garlic clove

BOURBON-GLAZED ONIONS
150g (1¼ cups) baby onions
2 white onions
Oil, for frying
A couple of shots of Bourbon whiskey
50g (3½ Tbsp) butter
200ml (¾ cup) chicken stock
A few sprigs of fresh thyme
2 garlic cloves

Add the chicken thighs to the BBQ sauce and marinate in an ovenproof dish for as long as you have but ideally overnight.

Peel the celeriac and dice half into 2cm (¾in) cubes and put to one side. Roughly chop the remainder of the celeriac for the puree. Place the celeriac for the puree in one pan with the milk and 100g (½ cup) of the butter and a pinch of salt. Cover with a round of baking paper and cook slowly until it starts to break up and the milk has reduced slightly. Blend in a blender until super smooth, season with salt and keep warm until later – if the puree looks grainy, add a small cube of cold butter and continue to blend.

Put the diced celeriac in a second pan with the stock, remaining 2 tablespoons of butter, thyme and garlic. Simmer the celeriac until tender but holding its shape. Leave in the stock until required.

Preheat the oven to 180°C (350°F) Gas 4. Put the marinated chicken in the oven and bake until sticky – this should take around 40 minutes. Remember to baste the thighs in the sauce every 10 minutes or so.

While the chicken is cooking, peel the onions. Soak the baby onions in warm water before peeling – this softens the skin allowing for an easier job. Peel the white onions and halve through the middle. Heat a frying pan to medium high with a drizzle of oil. Place the onion halves flat side down and allow to colour. Push the white onions to the back of the pan and place the baby onions in the front. Cook until all the onions are a deep colour then turn the white onions over and add the Bourbon to the pan. Take extra care when adding the alcohol as it will produce a flame – make sure you step back and are ready for it! Once the flames have died down add the butter, stock, thyme and garlic and bake for 20 minutes, or until the onions are super soft but holding their shape.

Serve in individual bowls at the table and tuck in or, if you're feeling creative and want to go the extra mile, spoon the puree onto the plate, add the chicken and the onion halves. Fill in all the gaps with the celeriac cubes and baby onions.

STICKY-ICKY BLACKENED LIME,

TEQUILA AND HONEY DRUMSTICKS

The first time we tried out this recipe was at Glastonbury Festival in 2017. Festival work is relentless – early mornings accepting deliveries and preparing food and then tossing wings and serving into the early hours. We put this together for a staff meal during the festival. It was simple, quick and used up ingredients we had to hand but it is now a firm staff favourite and often gets cooked when we get the original band back together.

Preheat the oven to 170°C (325°F) Gas 3.

Heat a griddle pan until it starts to smoke. Halve 3 of the limes and place cut sides down in the pan until they start to caramelize. Allow the natural sugars to catch in the pan and start to blacken.

In a small saucepan bring together the honey, brown sugar, 150ml (⅔ cup) water and the tequila. Grate in the lime zest from the remaining lime and squeeze in all of the juice from the blackened and fresh limes.

Place the drumsticks in a roasting pan and cover with three-quarters of the glaze and throw in the lime halves. Bake for 35–40 minutes until fully glazed and super sticky. Constantly baste during cooking with the reserved glaze to ensure the chicken stays super moist and takes on a deep caramel colour.

Serve in the roasting pan with the rest of the tequila for drinking!

SERVES 4

4 limes
200g (⅔ cup) honey
3 Tbsp soft dark brown sugar
Tequila, 2 shots for the sauce – one for the chef
8 chicken drumsticks

XO-GLAZED CHICKEN
WITH CHINESE BROCCOLI

XO sauce packs a punch and is one of those ingredients in Asian cookery that really adds depth to your food. This is one of those dishes that you throw together super quick but will deliver time and time again. If you can't get hold of Chinese broccoli change it up with Tenderstem broccoli (broccolini) or pak choi and the result will be just as good.

Cut the thighs down the middle and marinate in the XO, soy and sesame oil for at least 2 hours – ideally overnight – in the fridge.

Preheat the oven to 180°C (350°F) Gas 4. Place the thighs in a small roasting pan, shaping each one into a little oyster shape by tucking the ends underneath. Roast in the oven for 25–30 minutes.

Bring a large pan of salted water to a rapid boil. Add the broccoli or pak choi and cook for 3–4 minutes until the stems have just started to soften. Strain through a colander and allow to sit for a minute, ensuring all the water has drained.

Arrange the broccoli or pak choi on a large board or plate, add the chicken and any juices from the roasting pan. Sprinkle generously with the cashews and a few shakes of togarashi.

SERVES 4

6 skinless, boneless chicken thighs
2 Tbsp XO sauce
2 Tbsp light soy sauce
1 Tbsp sesame oil
400g (14oz) Chinese broccoli or
   pak choi (bok choy)

GARNISH
50g (½ cup) roasted crushed
   cashew nuts
Togarashi spice blend

CAJUN LIVER SLIDERS WITH BURNT

CORN MAYO AND CHICKEN-FAT ONIONS

SERVES 4

500g (1lb 2oz) chicken livers
200ml (scant 1 cup) whole milk
125g (¾ cup) plain (all-purpose) flour
5 Tbsp Cajun seasoning
8 mini (3in) sesame buns, halved
75g (5 Tbsp) butter, melted
Salt and black pepper

BURNT CORN MAYO

1 corn on the cob
Rapeseed (canola) oil, for frying
200ml (1 cup) mayonnaise
1 shallot, finely chopped
30g (1 cup) fresh coriander (cilantro),
   finely chopped

CHICKEN-FAT ONIONS

2 large white onions, thinly sliced
50g (3½ Tbsp) chicken fat
1 Tbsp fresh thyme leaves

Liver is not an ingredient that people cook much at home any more, but we want to change this. These tasty little morsels get hit with a pinch of spice but are offset by the sweet onions and charred corn. They're served up in a mini burger bun, because... who doesn't like a burger?!

Trim the chicken livers, removing any clusters of fat, discoloured patches or heavy veins. Slice the livers into flat pieces so they do not fold over during cooking. Soak in the milk in the fridge for a couple of hours to remove any impurities.

For the mayo, heat a griddle pan until smoking. Rub the corn in a little oil and sprinkle with salt. Add to the pan and allow to colour and brown on all sides before removing from the heat. Once the corn has cooled slightly, stand it on its end and run a knife down the cob removing all the kernels. Reserve a quarter of the kernels and add the remainder to a small food processor with the mayonnaise. Blend until smooth.

Place the shallot and coriander in a small bowl and stir through the corn mayo and the reserved kernels. Season with a little salt and pepper.

Cook the onions over a low heat in a small pan with the chicken fat and thyme until deep and rich in colour.

In a bowl combine the flour and Cajun seasoning. Drain the chicken livers and discard the milk. Toss the liver slices in the flour a few at a time and cook in a medium hot frying pan (skillet) for 2 minutes on each side. Repeat in batches, wiping out the pan every time, until they are all done.

Toast the buns in a dry pan and brush with the melted butter. Spoon the onions on the bottom of the bun and add the livers. Add the corn mayo to the top of the bun and sandwich together – boom!

MINI KIEVS WITH CREAMY
CHARRED LEEKS AND PANCETTA

For the garlic butter, mix all the ingredients together in a small container, season and place in the freezer until solid.

Remove any sinew from the chicken breasts and chop into 2.5cm (1in) pieces. Put in a food processor and blitz a few times until smooth and then add the egg whites, continuing to blend until fully worked in. Add the cream. To check the seasoning, boil a small pan of water and add a little spoon of the mix. The mixture should hold together and cook in a minute or so – check that it is white throughout with no pink showing. Taste and adjust the seasoning of the mix if needed.

Using a warm scoop, divide the garlic butter into 12 balls about 1 tablespoon in size, and place back in the freezer. Using wet hands, divide the chicken mixture into 12 even balls. Push the butter into the middle of each ball, smoothing the chicken evenly around it. Keep refrigerated until all done.

Set up three bowls: one with the flour, the second with the beaten eggs and milk, and the third with the panko breadcrumbs. Season the flour and breadcrumbs with salt and pepper. Pass the balls through the flour, eggs and breadcrumbs. Store in the fridge until ready to cook – it is important to ensure the crust is fully coated around the ball otherwise it may pop during cooking.

Split the leek in half lengthways and thoroughly wash to remove any dirt. Colour in a hot griddle pan until lightly charred. Remove the leek pieces and slice them. In a saucepan, sweat the pancetta in the butter until soft and lightly coloured, then add the leeks and the cream. Continue to cook until the cream has reduced.

Preheat a deep fryer to 175ºC (350ºF) and cook the balls for 6–7 minutes. These will be super-hot when they come out of the fryer, so be extremely careful.

Spoon a little of the leek mixture in the bottom of a serving dish and pop a Kiev ball on top. Take care when taking the first bite – if done correctly there will be a gush of butter that will be volcanic. Enjoy with caution!

MAKES 12 BALLS

2 large skinless, boneless chicken breasts
2 egg whites
100ml (scant ½ cup) double (heavy) cream
200g (1½ cups) plain (all-purpose) flour
2 eggs, beaten
100ml (scant ½ cup) whole milk
350g (8 cups) panko breadcrumbs
Salt and black pepper
2 or 3L (2 or 3qt) vegetable or rapeseed (canola) oil, for cooking

GARLIC BUTTER

250g (1 cup plus 2 Tbsp) butter, softened
4 garlic cloves, finely chopped
2 Tbsp freshly chopped parsley
1 Tbsp freshly chopped thyme leaves

CREAMY LEEKS AND PANCETTA

1 large leek
100g (scant ¾ cup) fine pancetta lardons
25g (1½ Tbsp) butter
100ml (scant ½ cup) double (heavy) cream

NOTE
Place the bowl and blade of a food processor in the freezer for an hour. This helps to keep the chicken cold and ensures the mix doesn't split during the blending process.

Here you are: a retro 70s classic brought up to date. There are a few steps to this recipe, but if you stick to them you will get the most satisfying result. Everybody remembers having chicken Kiev as a kid – making that initial cut through the chicken and watching the butter pour out of it. The idea of freezing the butter here helps you achieve that.

THE BIG FEED

If you could somehow incorporate a theme tune into a book, then this section would be introduced by 'Eye of the Tiger' from *Rocky*, on full blast.

Go big or go bird... The Big Feed represents our view on the ultimate chicken feast – perfect for dining with friends, family or large groups. When it comes to indulging in homemade comfort foods, the experience is as much to do with who you share it with as it is about the food itself.

THE O.G. CHOWDER

This is campfire food with a few bells and whistles. There's nothing better than a hot bowl of soup on a cold winter's day and this recipe embraces just that feeling. This is ideal as one big pot shared with mates. We once made this using 10 kilograms of chicken that we picked from chicken wings – if that's not a labour of love, we don't know what is!

To make the cob, combine the flours in a large mixing bowl. Add the salt to one side of the bowl and the instant yeast to the other. Add the butter and 240ml (1 cup) of the warm water and start bringing the mixture together with your fingers. Add more water a little at a time, until you've picked up all the flour from the sides of the bowl – you may not need to add all the water or you may need to add more, depending on the flour. The dough should be soft but not soggy. Use the mixture to clean the inside of the bowl, making sure to fold the edges into the middle. Keep going until the mixture forms a rough dough.

Coat the work surface with a little olive oil, tip the dough onto it and begin to knead. Knead for 5–10 minutes, until the dough starts to form a soft, smooth skin. When your dough feels smooth and silky, put it into a lightly oiled, large bowl. Cover with a dish towel and leave to rise until at least doubled in size.

Line a baking sheet with baking paper. Dust your work surface lightly with flour and tip your dough out. Knock the air out of the dough until it is smooth. Flatten the dough and fold it back into its centre – flip the dough over and cup underneath with both hands to tidy it up. Place it on the baking sheet.

Put the baking sheet into a clean plastic bag and leave for a second prove for about an hour or until the dough has doubled in size. Preheat the oven to 220°C (425°F) Gas 7, and put a baking sheet in the bottom to heat up. Dust the top of the loaf with flour and bake for 30 minutes – when cooked the loaf should sound hollow.

METHOD AND INGREDIENTS CONTINUED OVERLEAF...

SERVES 4

- 1 whole cooked small chicken, about 1.2kg (2¾lb)
- 1 white onion, diced
- Oil, for frying
- 500g (1lb 2oz) fresh clams
- 250ml (1 cup) white wine
- 1 leek, cut into 1cm (½in) pieces
- 2 celery sticks, cut into 1cm (½in) pieces
- 150g (¾ cup) smoked pancetta lardons
- 1 large floury potato, such as Maris Piper, peeled and cubed
- 1 small can of sweetcorn, about 200g (7oz)
- 1.75L (7 cups) chicken stock
- 1 bay leaf
- 2 sprigs of fresh thyme
- 200ml (scant 1 cup) double (heavy) cream
- ½ bunch of fresh chives, finely chopped
- 1 sheet of ready-rolled puff pastry, chilled
- 1 egg yolk

For the butter, add the cream to a mixer with a whisk attachment. Whisk until the mixture has split into two, leaving behind a watery liquid in the bottom of the bowl. Remove the pale stiffened butter from the whisk and form into a ball. Rinse the ball of butter under cold water. Shape into a log and wrap in baking paper until needed. When ready to serve, sprinkle with a little sea salt.

Strip the chicken from the bones and refrigerate until required. Sweat half the onions in a hot pan with a little oil until soft. Add the clams and allow to heat up, pour in the wine and pop on a lid. The clams are cooked when they fully open up. Discard any clams that do not open up after 4 minutes. Strain the clams through a sieve, making sure to keep the cooking liquid. Remove the clams from their shells and discard the shells. Refrigerate the clams.

In a large pan sweat the remaining onions with the leek, celery and lardons until soft. Add the reserved clam liquid and reduce. Add the potato to the pan with the sweetcorn and all its juices. Pour in the chicken stock and add the bay leaf and a sprig of thyme. Once the potato has cooked and the stock has reduced slightly, add the cream and remove from the heat.

Add the chicken and the clams to the chowder base and check the seasoning. Add the chives. Cool slightly before pouring into a deep ovenproof pot.

Preheat the oven to 180°C (350°F) Gas 4. Remove the puff pastry from the fridge and allow to warm up slightly. Roll out over the top of the chowder pot and trim any excess. Glaze the pastry with the egg yolk and place in the fridge. After 10 minutes glaze with the egg yolk a second time. Pick the leaves from the remaining thyme sprig and sprinkle over the pastry with a little sea salt.

Bake for 25 minutes or until the pastry has puffed up and taken on a deep golden colour. Serve immediately with all the bread, all the butter and all your mates.

COUNTRY COB
400g (3 cups) strong wholemeal (wholewheat) flour
100g (⅔ cup) strong white bread flour, plus extra for dusting
2 tsp salt
2 tsp instant yeast
40g (3 Tbsp) unsalted butter, softened
320ml (1⅓ cups) warm water
Olive oil, for kneading

FRESH BUTTER
250ml (1 cup) double (heavy) cream
Sea salt, to serve

MAPLE-GLAZED CHICKEN WITH ALL THE CORN

SERVES 6

1 whole chicken, about 1.8kg (4lb)
2 heads of garlic, halved horizontally
4 large shallots
2 carrots, halved
3 lemons, halved
2 celery sticks
Olive oil
200ml (scant 1 cup) maple syrup
Salt and black pepper
1 recipe Cornbread (see page 72),
　baked in a loaf pan

CREAMED CORN
2 shallots, chopped
1 garlic clove, chopped
Butter, for frying
2 small cans of sweetcorn, about 200g
　(7oz) each, drained
1 Tbsp dried thyme
150ml (⅔ cup) chicken stock
75ml (⅓ cup) double (heavy) cream
1 Tbsp freshly chopped parsley
100g (1½ cups) grated Parmesan cheese

MAPLE BACON BUTTER
2 rashers (slices) of smoked streaky
　bacon
Maple syrup
100g (½ cup minus 1 Tbsp) unsalted
　butter, softened

Your next Sunday lunch needs to be this simple. Ditch the traditional vegetables and mix it up a little. You don't need to be stuck in the kitchen all day to produce great results – have a crack at this one and let us know how you get on.

Preheat the oven to 190°C (375°F) Gas 5. Place the chicken on a board in front of you and run your knife down the back of the spine to open up the bird, enabling you to flatten it.

In the bottom of a roasting pan add the garlic halves, shallots, carrots, lemons and celery. Rub the chicken with olive oil, season with salt and pepper and place on top of the vegetables. Roast for 35–40 minutes, then pour over the maple syrup and cook for a further 10 minutes, basting regularly.

For the creamed corn, sweat the shallots and garlic in a pan with some butter until cooked but not coloured. Add the sweetcorn, thyme and stock, then bring to a simmer and reduce by two thirds. Add the cream, parsley and grated Parmesan. Season with salt and a generous amount of black pepper.

For the butter, chop the bacon into tiny lardons and render in a small pan. Once cooked and crispy, add a generous drizzle of maple syrup. Put the softened butter in a serving dish, creating a little well in the centre using a hot spoon. Fill with the bacon mix.

Load up your feast onto a few boards with the butter and some cornbread on the side. Knock up a batch of dirty iced tea and get stuck in.

TEA-BRINED BIRD, BUTTERED GREENS AND WHIPPED MASH

This is a little labour-intensive, but it will result in some of the most incredibly tender and moist chicken you are likely to taste. Don't be put off by the brining – it's simple once you get your head around it. If you're feeling creative, change up the spices you put in the brine. Add extra chillies if that's your thing, load it with herbs, or throw in extra citrus – there are no rules. Go crazy!

For the brine, mix 500ml (2 cups) water, the peppercorns, salt, sugar, seeds, bay leaf and tea in a saucepan. Bring everything to the boil and continue to boil until the salt and sugar dissolves completely. Cool the mixture. Put your chicken in a large resealable bag. Add the cooled brine along with the whole shallots and 3 of the garlic-head halves. Seal the bag, making sure to force as much air out as possible and pop in the fridge for a day.

Preheat the oven to 170°C (325°F) Gas 3. Remove the chicken from the brine and pat dry, inside and out. In a roasting pan, create a bed for the chicken to sit on with the carrots, celery, shallots, thyme and the last garlic-head half. Drizzle the chicken with a generous amount of olive oil and a few twists of pepper. Roast in the oven until the juices run clear, approximately 70–80 minutes. Once cooked, pour off the roasting juices into a small container.

Boil the potatoes in salted water. When tender, strain off the water and return the potatoes to the pan over a low heat until the excess water has evaporated. At this point whisk in the butter, marrow and the milk and beat until smooth. Season and keep warm.

Heat a deep, large saucepan for the greens, add half the butter and the greens and season with salt and pepper. Add a splash of water to create some steam and put a lid on top. Shake the pan every minute or so, to ensure the greens steam and soften rather than fry. Once soft but with retained colour, add the rest of the butter and taste for seasoning.

Serve the greens alongside the chicken, potatoes and reserved roasting juices.

SERVES 6

1 whole chicken, about 1.8kg (4lb)
2 carrots, chopped
2 celery sticks, chopped
3 shallots, chopped
Small bunch of fresh thyme
Olive oil, for basting
Salt and black pepper

BRINE
10 black peppercorns
4 Tbsp sea salt
1 Tbsp brown sugar
1 tsp yellow mustard seeds
1 tsp coriander seeds
1 bay leaf
30g (5 Tbsp) loose smoked Earl Grey tea leaves
2 large shallots
2 heads of garlic, unpeeled and cut in half

BUTTERED GREENS
25g (1½ Tbsp) butter
500g (1lb 2oz) seasonal greens, shredded

WHIPPED BONE MARROW POTATOES
5 large floury potatoes, such as Maris Piper, cubed
200g (1 cup) butter
100g (3½oz) bone marrow melt
3 Tbsp milk

NOTE
The day before you plan to cook this recipe you will need to brine your chicken. This simply means submerging your chicken in liquid to impart flavour and to tenderize it – it's nothing to be scared of...

GRILLED CHICKEN SHAWARMA WITH ALL THE TRIMMINGS

This is the ultimate Middle Eastern feast for you, your family and friends. Bring this to the table and it will satisfy every time. Some of the best memories are made sharing meals with great company, laughing and joking over plates piled high with food. This incredible recipe gives you just the platform to do that.

To prepare the shawarma, blend all the ingredients except the chicken together until smooth and work into the chicken thighs, ensuring they are all covered with the marinade. Thread the meat onto 2 long metal skewers, ensuring any bits of meat that are hanging off are tucked in between the layers of thigh. Keep refrigerated until needed.

Chop the cucumber, tomatoes and red onion for the salad into even 1cm (½in) dice. Add the spring onions and parsley and then dress with the lemon juice, a drizzle of olive oil, and some salt and pepper.

Mix the red onions with the sumac, lemon juice and oil.

For the flatbreads, mix the flour and baking powder in a bowl and make a well in the centre. Pour the yogurt into the middle, add a pinch of salt and start to bring together using your fingers. Work the dough until it is soft but no longer sticky. Divide the dough into walnut-sized balls. Stretch out each ball until the size of a side plate (about 15cm/6in diameter). Cook on a dry griddle pan on either side until coloured and slightly charred. Brush with the butter and a rub of garlic.

SERVES 8

3 Tbsp ground cumin
5 Tbsp ground coriander
½ bunch of fresh coriander (cilantro)
Bunch of fresh mint
½ bunch of fresh parsley
300ml (1½ cups) natural (plain) yogurt
5 garlic cloves
Salt and black pepper
18 chicken thighs, skin on

MIXED SALAD
1 cucumber
4 tomatoes
1 red onion
3 spring onions (scallions), sliced
Handful of fresh parsley, chopped
Freshly squeezed juice of ½ lemon
Olive oil

SUMAC RED ONIONS
2 red onions, sliced
1 Tbsp sumac
Freshly squeezed juice of ½ lemon
2 Tbsp olive oil

MINI FLATBREADS
400g (3 cups) plain (all-purpose) flour
400ml (2 cups) natural (plain) yogurt
2 tsp baking powder
100g (½ cup minus 1 Tbsp) butter, melted
1 garlic clove, halved

TO SERVE
50g (½ cup) chopped pistachios
Seeds from ½ pomegranate
4 radishes, sliced
Roasted chickpeas (garbanzo beans), optional
Regret It in the Morning Sauce (see page 179), a small serving
Roasted Garlic Houmous (see page 185)
Zaatar Tahini (see page 185)

Get the BBQ (grill) fired up and ensure that the flames have died off before cooking this bad boy! Place each chicken skewer with one side facing down and allow the meat to slowly cook and colour underneath. Once the meat has coloured turn over to the other side and repeat the process. Continue this on all sides, remembering to baste with the leftover marinade.

If cooking in an oven, preheat the oven to 170°C (325°F) Gas 3. Place the shawarma on a baking sheet lined with vegetables (e.g. onions, garlic and peppers) and bake for 45–50 minutes, basting throughout. The chicken should reach a minimum of 75°C (170°F) in the centre.

Lay the shawarma on a large board and scatter with the pistachios and pomegranate seeds. Pile on the salads, radishes, roasted chickpeas, sauce, houmous, zaatar tahini and flatbreads. The rest is simple!

NOTE
This dish can be cooked either on a BBQ (grill) or in the oven – for best results and we really do mean best results, get it outdoors on the BBQ!

Veggie

The concept of Wingmans was born and bred on the street-food and festival circuit where our main goal was to be able to cater for the majority. While it is a chicken-focused concept, a Wingman never leaves anyone behind.

Whatever your dietary requirements, we have always got you covered!

On top of that, Mama always taught us to eat our greens, so this chapter is for everyone!

Shanghai Cauliflower

As a main course or a side dish to share, this will have meat-eaters immediately upping their veggie intake. Sweet, rich and super crunchy, this is a winner every time.

Mix the soy yogurt with the spices and seasonings. Mix the flours together in a separate bowl. Pass the cauliflower florets through the yogurt mix into the flour, making sure to fully coat each floret.

Preheat a deep fryer to 170°C (325°F) and cook the cauliflower for 8 minutes. Cook in batches so the florets do not stick together.

Toss the crispy cauliflower with the Shanghai sauce and the sesame seeds. Arrange in a serving dish. Garnish with the chilli, spring onions and coriander, with the mayonnaise alongside, if you like.

SERVES 4

150ml (¾ cup) soy-based yogurt
1 Tbsp Chinese five spice
2 tsp celery salt
2 tsp white pepper
1 tsp black pepper
250g (2½ cups) cornflour (cornstarch)
50g (⅓ cup) rice flour
2 cauliflowers, divided into medium-sized florets
2 or 3L (2 or 3qt) vegetable or rapeseed (canola) oil, for cooking
200ml (scant 1 cup) Shanghai Sauce (see page 174)
1 Tbsp black sesame seeds, toasted
1 Tbsp white sesame seeds, toasted

GARNISH

1 fresh red chilli, finely sliced
Bunch of spring onions (scallions), green tops only, finely shredded
A few sprigs of fresh coriander (cilantro), leaves picked
50ml (¼ cup) Japanese mayonnaise (optional)

Sometimes it takes little to no effort to change the flavour of a dish. Charring broccoli completely does this. If you're feeling adventurous, try it on a BBQ.

Blackened Broccoli and Louisiana Red Pepper Hot Sauce with Salsa Verde

SERVES 2

1 head of broccoli
100ml (scant ½ cup) olive oil
Salt and black pepper

LOUISIANA RED PEPPER HOT SAUCE
2 red (bell) peppers
200g (1½ cups) fresh red chilli, chopped
1 fresh red Scotch bonnet, stem removed (wear gloves, these are seriously hot!), chopped
1 white onion, chopped
2 garlic cloves, chopped
Oil, for frying
4 Tbsp caster (granulated) sugar
150ml (⅔ cup) white wine vinegar

SALSA VERDE
100g (3½oz) gherkins (about 5 whole)
100g (½ cup) capers
Small bunch of fresh parsley
Small bunch of fresh mint
4 Tbsp red wine vinegar
2 tsp mild Dijon mustard
175ml (¾ cup) olive oil

TO SERVE
1 shallot, sliced
50ml (¼ cup) white wine vinegar
1 Tbsp caster (granulated) sugar
1 lime, halved

Preheat the oven to 180°C (350°F) Gas 4. Trim the base of the broccoli then, with a large sharp knife, cut into two portions. Place each half flat side down on a chopping board and trim so that both sides are flat. Rub the inside of the broccoli head with the oil and season.

Heat a griddle pan and sear the broccoli for a couple of minutes on both sides, then finish cooking in the oven for 12–15 minutes.

For the hot sauce, using a blowtorch, blister the skins of the peppers until black. Place in a bowl and cover in clingfilm (plastic wrap). Leave to cool. Peel the skins off the peppers and discard with the seeds. Chop the peppers and put to one side.

Sweat the chillies, onion and garlic with a little oil in a pan until soft, then add the roasted peppers, sugar and vinegar. Cook until the vinegar has reduced by half. Cool slightly then pour into a mini blender and pulse until the sauce comes together.

Put all the ingredients for the salsa verde into a food processor, except the olive oil. Pulse until fully chopped. Scrape out into a bowl and slowly add the olive oil. Season with salt and black pepper.

Pickle the shallot in the vinegar and sugar for at least 20 minutes before serving. Meanwhile, heat a griddle pan. Place the lime halves flat side down in the pan. Allow the natural sugars in the lime to caramelize and turn a deep colour.

Pop it all on plates and enjoy your spicy vegan creation!

Oyster Mushroom Tempura with Curry Leaf Mayo

VEGGIE

Sometimes the simple things are the best – and this recipe is exactly that. Enjoy!

For the mayo, add the curry leaves to the olive oil in a small saucepan. Warm slightly and leave to infuse. Strain off when the oil takes on the flavour of the leaves.

Mix together the egg yolks, turmeric, mustard and vinegar in a bowl. Slowly whisk in the flavoured oil. Toast the mustard seeds and add to the mayonnaise. Season with salt and pepper.

Preheat a deep fryer to 190ºC (375ºF). Mix the cornflour with a good pinch of salt. Whisk in the sparkling water and drop in the ice cubes to keep it cold. The mixture should be like a thin cream. Dip the mushrooms into the batter mix and deep-fry until golden and crisp.

Dust the tempura with the Szechuan seasoning and serve hot with the curry mayo.

SERVES 4

400g (4 cups) cornflour (cornstarch)
150ml (⅔ cup) sparkling water
3 ice cubes
500g (1lb 2oz) oyster mushrooms
2 or 3L (2 or 3qt) vegetable or rapeseed (canola) oil, for cooking
Szechuan seasoning, to taste
Salt and black pepper

CURRY LEAF MAYO
8 curry leaves
250ml (1 cup) light olive oil
2 egg yolks
½ tsp ground turmeric
1 tsp Dijon mustard
75ml (⅓ cup) rice wine vinegar
1 tsp brown mustard seeds

Sweetcorn Drop Cakes with Avocado, Sticky Onions and Jalapeño Sour Cream

To make the batter for the drop cakes, blend all of the ingredients together, except the oil, in a food processor and keep chilled until required.

Add the jalapeños to the sour cream, stir in the lime juice and zest. Season and set aside.

Peel the baby onions and colour in a hot frying pan (skillet) in a little oil. Add the butter, sugar and a splash of water. Cook until the onions are soft and sticky – add a splash of water to the pan if the glaze over reduces.

Heat up a large non-stick frying pan with a little oil in the bottom and spoon in 3 tablespoons of batter per drop cake. The drop cake is ready to flip when it starts to bubble around the edge and has turned a lovely golden-brown colour. Continue in batches with the rest of the mixture.

Scoop out the avocado and crush lightly, seasoning with the salt, pepper and lime juice. Stack up the drop cakes, load with the crushed avocado, jalapeño sour cream and sticky onions. Finish with a scattering of chilli and coriander.

SERVES 2

60g (⅓ cup) plain (all-purpose) flour
1 tsp baking powder
2 eggs
1 x 400g (14oz) can of sweetcorn
1 spring onion (scallion)
Oil, for frying
Salt and black pepper

JALAPEÑO SOUR CREAM

2 pickled jalapeños, chopped
100ml (scant ½ cup) sour cream
Freshly squeezed juice and zest
  of 1 lime

STICKY ONIONS

250g (2½ cups) baby onions
50g (3½ Tbsp) butter
100g (½ cup) soft dark brown sugar

TO SERVE

1 avocado
¾ tsp salt
½ tsp black pepper
Freshly squeezed juice of ½ lime

GARNISH

½ fresh red chilli, sliced
A few sprigs of fresh coriander (cilantro)

This is true comfort food, piled high with all the extra bells and whistles. It's an easy option for breakfast, brunch, lunch or dinner, and it will make even the fussiest eater happy.

Crispy Melty Mozzarella Bombs with Caramelized Onion Mayo and Tomato Jam

SERVES 4

4 field mushrooms
2 sprigs of thyme, leaves only
1 garlic clove, sliced
Light olive oil, for drizzling
4 mozzarella balls
100g (½ cup) pesto
150g (1 cup) plain (all-purpose) flour
2 eggs, beaten
250g (6 cups) panko breadcrumbs
Salt and black pepper
2 or 3L (2 or 3qt) vegetable or rapeseed
  (canola) oil, for cooking

CARAMELIZED ONION MAYO
1 white onion
50g (¼ cup) caster (granulated) sugar
200ml (1 cup) mayonnaise

BALSAMIC TOMATO JAM
2 tomatoes, chopped
1 white onion, chopped
2 garlic cloves, chopped
50ml (¼ cup) balsamic vinegar
2 Tbsp soft dark brown sugar

TO SERVE
4 sesame buns, halved
60g (3 cups) rocket (arugula)

For the caramelized onion mayo, slice the onion and sweat in a pan until a deep brown colour. Add the sugar and continue to caramelize. Cool the onions slightly and blend with the mayonnaise in a food processor until fairly smooth.

Preheat the oven to 170ºC (325ºF) Gas 3.

For the jam, sweat the tomatoes, onion and garlic in a pan together. Add the balsamic vinegar and the sugar then reduce to a jam-like consistency – about 20 minutes.

Arrange the mushrooms on a baking sheet and scatter over the thyme, garlic, and some salt and pepper. Drizzle with olive oil. Roast in the oven for 15–20 minutes.

Preheat a deep fryer to 170ºC (325ºF). Cut through (but not all the way through) the mozzarella balls, scoop out a little hole in the middle and stuff with the pesto. Close them up again. Put the flour, egg and breadcrumbs in three separate bowls. Roll the mozzarella through the flour, egg and breadcrumbs, ensuring the breadcrumbs completely coat the surface. Deep-fry until golden – about 4 minutes.

For each serving, toast the bun and spoon some jam on the bottom. Add a roasted mushroom, some rocket and a mozzarella bomb. Spoon the onion mayo on the top bun and squeeze everything together.

THINGS TO GO WITH WINGS

Every chick has a side chick and here is a selection of some of our personal favourites.

From our legendary mac & cheese to charred corn and everything in between, these mouthwatering sides are everything you need to satisfy you in life.

TRUFFLE BUTTER AND PARMESAN FRIES

Mix the butter and the finely chopped truffle and truffle oil together until well combined, then season with salt, to taste.

Preheat a deep fryer to 190°C (375°F) and cook the French fries until golden brown, crunchy and fluffy.

Toss the fries in the truffle butter and season with a pinch of salt. Generously sprinkle over the grated Parmesan and serve piping hot!

SERVES 4

100g (½ cup minus 1 Tbsp) butter, softened

20g (¾oz) black truffle, very finely chopped

2 or 3L (2 or 3qt) vegetable or rapeseed (canola) oil, for cooking

2 tsp white truffle oil

600g (1lb 5oz) frozen French fries

100g (1½ cups) grated Parmesan cheese, to serve

Salt

'NDUJA BABY POTATOES

MAPLE SWEET POTATO FRIES

SERVES 4

500g (3½ cups) new potatoes
2 or 3L (2 or 3qt) vegetable or rapeseed
   (canola) oil, for cooking
Salt and black pepper
½ recipe of Slow-Roasted Garlic Mayo
   (see page 182), to serve

'NDUJA BUTTER
50g (3½ Tbsp) butter
100g (¾ cup) 'nduja

CHIMICHURRI
100g (5 cups) fresh mint
100g (5 cups) fresh parsley
150g (6 cups) fresh coriander (cilantro)
50g (2 cups) fresh oregano
100ml (scant ½ cup) red wine vinegar
200ml (scant 1 cup) olive oil
1 shallot, finely chopped
2 fresh red chillies, finely chopped
3 garlic cloves, finely chopped

Parboil the potatoes in salted water for about 10 minutes. Drain and leave to cool. Give each potato a little squeeze and flatten slightly.

Put the butter in a small pan and crumble in the 'nduja. Allow the butter and 'nduja to melt down together then bring to the boil. Once boiled, remove from the heat and set aside.

For the chimichurri, pulse the herbs, vinegar and oil together in a food processor. Spoon into a bowl and add the shallot, chilli and garlic. Adjust the vinegar and olive oil as needed. Season well.

Preheat a deep fryer to 180°C (350°F) and lower in the potatoes. Cook until crispy. Arrange the potatoes in a serving dish and top off with the butter, chimichurri and slow-roasted garlic mayo.

SERVES 4

2 or 3L (2 or 3qt) vegetable or rapeseed
   (canola) oil, for cooking
600g (1lb 5oz) sweet potatoes, cut into long,
   1cm (½in) wide batons
200g (2 cups) potato starch
1 tsp caster (granulated) sugar
1 tsp smoked paprika
100ml (scant ½ cup) maple syrup, to serve

PECAN SALT
50g (½ cup) pecans, chopped
50g (¼ cup) sea salt

For the pecan salt, toast the pecans in a dry pan until charred around the edges. Blitz in a food processor with the sea salt and put to one side until required.

Preheat a deep fryer to 150°C (300°F). Lower in the sweet potatoes and cook for 3–4 minutes. Remove from the oil and spread out on a baking sheet to cool.

Mix the potato starch with the sugar and the smoked paprika and increase the temperature of the oil in the fryer to 180°C (350°F). In small batches, toss the cooled fries in the flour mix and fry until golden and crunchy.

Finish with a drizzle of maple syrup and sprinkled with the pecan salt.

SMOKEY BEANS WITH DIRTY GARLIC AND PAPRIKA

Place the head of garlic in the open fire if cooking on coals. Cook the chopped garlic (if cooking on a stove), onion, carrot and celery, over a medium heat and allow to brown around the edges. Add the paprika and tomato puree with a little splash of water, if needed to loosen. Once the paprika and tomato puree have cooked down, add the chicken stock and the block of pancetta. Simmer the liquid for 1 hour over a low heat.

Remove the pancetta from the liquid and allow it to cool. Remove and discard the skin, then shred the meat and set aside. Add the two cans of beans to the liquid and continue to cook until thick and sticky.

Stir in the shredded pancetta and the parsley. If the beans are too thick, add a little splash of water. Season and spoon into a serving bowl. Squeeze some of the dirty roasted garlic on the top (if cooked outdoors) and sprinkle with the toasted breadcrumbs.

SERVES 4

1 head of garlic if cooking on an open fire, or 3 garlic cloves, chopped (see Note)
1 white onion, chopped
1 carrot, chopped
2 celery sticks, chopped
2 Tbsp sweet smoked paprika
2 Tbsp tomato puree (paste)
1L (4 cups) chicken stock
250g (9oz) block of fatty pancetta
1 x 400g (14oz) can of white cannellini beans, drained
1 x 400g (14oz) can haricot (navy) beans, drained
3 Tbsp freshly chopped parsley
4 Tbsp toasted breadcrumbs

NOTE
If you're attempting this on an open fire, allow the flames to die down, then nuzzle the garlic between the coals and allow it to cook slowly in the skins – this little addition completely changes this recipe! Don't worry though – you can still get great results by cooking the garlic with the onions at the beginning of the recipe; if you're doing this, only use 3 cloves.

MAC & CHEESE WITH SHORT RIB AND CRACK CRUMB

Preheat the oven to 85°C (185°F) Gas ¼.

Seal the beef ribs in a hot frying pan (skillet) in a little oil until coloured on all sides. Place the ribs in an ovenproof dish and add the rest of the ingredients, mixing well. Cook in the oven overnight until the meat falls off the bone.

Remove the meat from the cooking liquid and strain the liquid into a saucepan. Bring to the boil and reduce by half. Pick the meat from the ribs and discard the bones and excess fat. Add the meat back to the sauce and reduce until thick and sticky.

Meanwhile, cook the pasta until al dente and refresh under cold water to stop the cooking.

Melt the butter in a pan and add the flour. Slowly add the milk and continually whisk to create a white sauce. Add all the cheeses to the sauce with the mustard, stirring until melted and the sauce has thickened. Season to taste.

For the crumb, sweat the garlic with the butter in a frying pan until translucent. Add the breadcrumbs and cook until they take on a deep brown colour. Crush the crisps and add to the breadcrumbs. Add the chives into the crumb and mix everything together.

Combine the pasta with the cheese sauce and check the seasoning. Build the mac and cheese by spooning the beef mixture into the bottom of the dish, adding the pasta and finishing with the crumb. Serve straightaway.

SERVES 4

300g (2 cups) short elbow pasta (macaroni)
100g (½ cup minus 1 Tbsp) butter
100g (⅔ cup) plain (all-purpose) flour
600ml (2½ cups) milk
250g (2¾ cups) grated Cheddar cheese
150g (1⅓ cups) grated mozzarella
100g (1½ cups) grated Parmesan cheese
2 Tbsp English mustard
Salt and black pepper

BEEF SHORT RIBS
2 beef short ribs, about 1.25kg (2lb 12oz) on the bone
Olive oil, for frying
1 fresh lemongrass stalk
¼ bunch of fresh coriander (cilantro), chopped
200g (2 cups) fresh root ginger, chopped
½ head of garlic
1L (4 cups) Shanghai Sauce (see page 174)
500ml (2 cups) Wingmans BBQ Sauce (see page 40)

CRACK CRUMB
1 garlic clove, chopped
150g (½ cup plus 2 Tbsp) butter
200g (4½ cups) panko breadcrumbs
1 packet roast chicken flavour crisps (chips)
½ bunch of fresh chives, chopped

BANG BANG BON BONS

MAKES 16 BALLS

1 small, whole smoked cooked chicken, about 1–1.2kg (2¼–2¾lb)
150ml (⅔ cup) Wingmans BBQ Sauce (see page 40)
100g (⅔ cup) plain (all-purpose) flour
2 eggs, beaten
100ml (scant ½ cup) milk
300g (7 cups) panko breadcrumbs
1 Tbsp garlic granules
2 Tbsp freshly chopped parsley
Sea salt and black pepper
2 or 3L (2 or 3qt) vegetable or rapeseed (canola) oil, for cooking

BANG-BANG DIP

1 shallot, finely chopped
1 garlic clove, chopped
½ fresh lemongrass stalk
1 Tbsp Madras curry powder
1 x 400ml (14fl oz) can of coconut milk
1 Tbsp chopped fresh red chilli
2 Tbsp peanut butter
50g (½ cup) roasted crushed peanuts
1 Tbsp sliced spring onion (scallion)

Pick and shred all the meat from the chicken. Combine it with the BBQ sauce, adding it slowly so as not to make it too wet. The mixture should be workable and firm enough to be able to form round balls. Season if needed.

Set up 3 bowls with the flour in one, the eggs and milk in a second and the third with the breadcrumbs, garlic and parsley. Pass the balls through the flour, egg mixture and breadcrumbs, ensuring they are completely coated.

Sweat the shallot with the garlic and lemongrass in a little oil. Add the Madras powder and cook for a couple of minutes, taking care not to burn the spices. Add the coconut milk and chilli and bring to the boil. Reduce slightly and remove from the heat. Add the peanut butter, peanuts and spring onions. Season and spoon into a serving dish.

Preheat a deep fryer to 180°C (350°F) and cook the bon bons in batches until golden brown. The centre of the bon bons should be over 75°C (170°F) when cooked. Season with some sea salt and arrange on a serving dish with the dip. Banging!

TRUFFLED MAC & CHEESE BALLS

Cook the pasta until al dente and refresh under cold water to stop the cooking.

Melt the butter in a pan and add the flour. Slowly add the milk and continually whisk to create a white sauce. Add all the cheeses to the sauce with the mustard, stirring until melted and the sauce has thickened. Stir in the truffle paste and oil at the end and season to taste.

Combine the pasta with the cheese sauce and pour into a container. Refrigerate until cold.

Set up 3 bowls for the coating: one with flour, one with eggs and milk and one with the breadcrumbs and garlic granules.

Once the macaroni is cold, shape it into balls and roll in the flour, egg wash and the garlic breadcrumbs.

Preheat a deep fryer to 170°C (350°F). Cook the balls until golden. Season with a little sea salt and serve with Buttermilk Ranch dressing.

MAKES 16 BALLS

600g (4½ cups) short elbow pasta (macaroni)
100g (½ cup minus 1 Tbsp) butter
100g (⅔ cup) plain (all-purpose) flour
600ml (2½ cups) milk
250g (2¾ cups) grated Cheddar cheese
150g (1⅓ cups) grated mozzarella
100g (1½ cups) grated Parmesan cheese
2 Tbsp English mustard
100g (7 Tbsp) truffle paste
2 Tbsp white truffle oil
Salt and black pepper
2 or 3L (2 or 3qt) vegetable or rapeseed (canola) oil, for cooking

COATING
100g (⅔ cup) plain (all-purpose) flour
2 eggs, beaten
100ml (scant ½ cup) milk
300g (7 cups) panko breadcrumbs
1 Tbsp garlic granules

TO SERVE
½ recipe Buttermilk Ranch dressing (see page 183), to serve

THE HAMSTRING

Thinly slice the onions into rings on a mandolin. Soak the sliced onions in the buttermilk for 30 minutes. Add the seasonings to the cornflour.

Preheat a deep fryer to 170°C (325°F). Toss the onions through the flour and fry immediately until crispy but still pale in colour. Drain on paper towels and season with a touch of sea salt.

Chop the bacon into small lardons. Cook in a small pan until rendered and crispy then add the honey, sugar and rosemary. Bring to the boil and reduce until thick and syrupy.

Spoon the honeyed bacon over the onions and devour!

SERVES 4

4 white onions
300ml (1¼ cups) buttermilk
1 tsp cayenne pepper
1 tsp black pepper
3 tsp sea salt
400g (4 cups) cornflour (cornstarch)
2 or 3L (2 or 3qt) vegetable or rapeseed (canola) oil, for cooking

HONEYED BACON
4 rashers (slices) of smoked streaky bacon
2 Tbsp honey
2 Tbsp light brown sugar
1 tsp freshly chopped rosemary

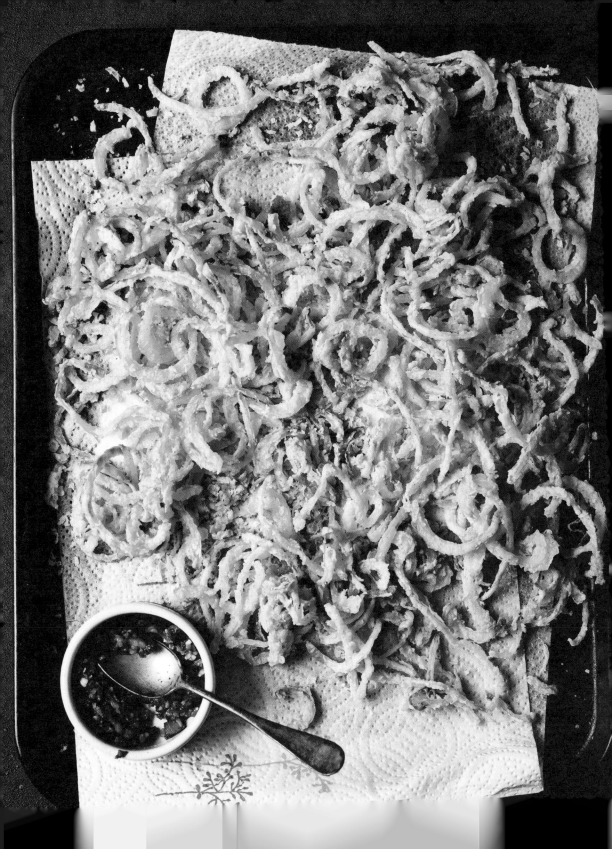

PICKLED KOHLRABI WITH FENNEL AND MUSTARD SEEDS

SERVES 4

2 star anise
1 tsp pink peppercorns
1 tsp black peppercorns
1 Tbsp coriander seeds
1 Tbsp mustard seeds
1 Tbsp fennel seeds
200g (1 cup) caster (granulated) sugar
300ml (1¼ cups) distilled white vinegar
2 kohlrabi, peeled and cut into thin
   chunks

Add all the ingredients except the kohlrabi to a pan with 100ml (scant ½ cup) water and bring to the boil. Once the sugar has dissolved pour the sauce over the kohlrabi.

Leave to pickle, ideally overnight; however, the longer you leave this one the better.

Clockwise from top left: Korean Cucumbers with Sesame Dressing; Green Papaya and Ginger Pickle; and Pickled Kohlrabi with Fennel and Mustard Seeds

KOREAN CUCUMBERS
WITH SESAME DRESSING

Halve the cucumbers lengthways and remove the seeds using a tablespoon. Cut into chunks.

Mix the gochujang with the vinegar, sugar, sesame seeds and sesame oil and add to the cucumbers. Leave to pickle overnight. The cucumbers will start to turn a deeper green when ready and will shrivel slightly but remain crunchy.

Spoon into a serving dish and drizzle with sesame dressing to serve.

SERVES 4

2 cucumbers
4 Tbsp gochujang (red chilli paste)
150ml (⅔ cup) distilled white vinegar
3 Tbsp caster (granulated) sugar
2 Tbsp black sesame seeds
2 Tbsp sesame oil
2 Tbsp Roasted Sesame Dressing
(see page 174), to serve

GREEN PAPAYA AND GINGER PICKLE

SERVES 4

1 green papaya
250g (8oz) daikon, peeled and finely
    grated
2 carrots, peeled and finely grated
1 red (bell) pepper, thinly sliced
½ green (bell) pepper, thinly sliced
200ml (scant 1 cup) rice vinegar
1 fresh red chilli, deseeded and thinly
    sliced
25g (3 Tbsp) peeled and grated fresh
    root ginger
100g (½ cup) caster (granulated) sugar

Peel the papaya, halve it and remove the seeds. Grate the flesh into a bowl with the daikon, carrots and peppers.

Stir in the vinegar, chilli, ginger and sugar. Leave to pickle for 48 hours in the fridge in an airtight container until the flavours have all developed.

APPLE, CHICORY AND RADISH SLAW

Using an apple corer, remove the core from the apple, halve and slice thinly. Peel the carrot and use a speed peeler to create ribbons.

Separate the leaves from the chicory and arrange in a bowl with the apple, vegetables and coriander. Pour in the dressing and toss at the last minute at the table to ensure everything stays crispy.

SERVES 4

1 Granny Smith apple
1 large carrot
1 chicory (endive)
150g (5½oz) red cabbage, shredded
250g (9oz) white cabbage, shredded
1 fresh red chilli, sliced
3 radishes, sliced
1 spring onion (scallion), sliced
A few large sprigs of fresh coriander (cilantro), leaves picked
150ml (⅔ cup) Roasted Sesame Dressing (see page 174), to serve

HOT CHILLI
TURNIPS

Heat the oil in a non-stick pan and sauté the ginger and garlic, until slightly golden. Add the spices and fry for a few seconds. Add the salt and mix well.

Add the turnips to the pan, mix well and cook for 3–4 minutes. Remove from the heat, add the vinegar and set aside to cool completely. Store for up to a month in the fridge in an airtight container.

SERVES 4

6 Tbsp mustard oil
3 Tbsp finely chopped fresh root ginger
2 Tbsp chopped garlic
1½ Tbsp mustard powder
1½ Tbsp Kashmiri red chilli powder
1½ Tbsp garam masala
2 Tbsp salt
500g (1lb 2oz) turnips, peeled and
    chopped into 5mm (¼in) chunks
3 Tbsp malt vinegar

CHARRED CORN WITH GOCHUJANG BUTTER

SERVES 4

A few sprigs of fresh coriander (cilantro)
1 fresh red chilli, halved
Hazelnut-sized piece of fresh root
    ginger, chopped
2 corn on the cob
Oil
Quick Pickled Cucumber (see page 184),
    to serve

GOCHUJANG BUTTER
1 Tbsp gochujang (red chilli paste)
50g (3½ Tbsp) butter, softened

TOGARASHI SALT
1 Tbsp togarashi spice blend
2 Tbsp sea salt

Bring a pan of water to the boil with the coriander, halved red chilli and chopped ginger. Add the corn and cook until al dente. Remove the corn from the pan and leave to cool. Slice each corn cob into 6 pieces.

Heat a griddle pan and brush each piece of corn with a little oil. Add to the pan and allow the corn to char around the edges.

Work the gochujang into the butter and pop into a serving dish. Mix the togarashi and the salt together.

Arrange the charred corn in a small dish and spoon over a little of the butter. Sprinkle with the flavoured salt and pop on some pickled cucumbers.

CHARRED CAVOLO NERO WITH CRISPY ANCHOVIES

Chop the cavolo nero into large pieces, discarding the stems and woody core from the leaves and wash thoroughly. Allow to drain and then pat dry. Coat the leaves in half the oil and lightly season.

Fry the garlic slices in a little oil until they take on a pale brown colour and are crispy. Remove and drain on some paper towels.

Fry the anchovies in the remaining olive oil. Add the breadcrumbs and stir everything together. Sauté the anchovy crumbs until golden brown.

Heat a griddle pan until smoking and cook the cavolo nero leaves, allowing them to char slightly.

Arrange the leaves on a plate and sprinkle with the anchovy crumb and garlic slices.

SERVES 4

2 large heads of cavolo nero
100ml (scant ½ cup) olive oil
2 garlic cloves, thinly sliced
50g (5 Tbsp) anchovies, chopped
100g (2⅓ cups) panko breadcrumbs
Salt and black pepper

LOADED GEM

Preheat the oven to 180°C (350°F) Gas 4. Stretch the chicken skins out on a baking sheet lined with baking paper. Season with salt and pepper and cook in the oven for about 10 minutes until golden and crisp. At the same time cook the bacon in a frying pan (skillet) until crispy.

Fry the bread cubes in the same pan after the bacon, adding a little olive oil.

Make the dressing by mixing together the mustard, oil, vinegar and honey, then season with a pinch of salt.

Remove the larger leaves from the lettuce and set aside. Finely shred the heart of the lettuce and place in a bowl. Crush in the bacon, crispy skins and the sliced and crispy onions. Add a little dressing and check the seasoning.

Load this mix into the lettuce leaves and arrange on a plate. Add the croutons and sprinkle over the Parmesan. Finish with an extra drizzle of the dressing.

MAKES 6 PIECES

100g (3½oz) chicken skins – about 4 skins
2 rashers (slices) of smoked bacon
1 slice of white bread, crusts removed and cut into 1cm (½in) cubes
Olive oil, for frying
2 baby gem lettuce
½ red onion, thinly sliced
4 Tbsp crispy onions
100g (1½ cups) grated Parmesan cheese
Salt and black pepper

DRESSING

1 Tbsp wholegrain mustard
125ml (½ cup) olive oil
4 Tbsp cider vinegar
2 Tbsp honey

HITTING THAT SWEET SPOT

If you have made it this far with room for dessert then you are a winner in our eyes and have earned our five most decadent recipes to date. Whether you are a chocoholic, crazy about crumble or prefer a more fruity alternative, we've got something for you — just make sure you don't tell your dentist.

"FALLIN' OFF THE WAGON" WHEEL

We have finally found a good use for those dry, leftover crispbreads – decadent wagon wheels! We've been making these for a long time and they get better every time. Stick to the recipe and DM us your creations.

Preheat the oven to 180°C (350°F) Gas 4.

For the base sponge, whisk the egg whites and caster sugar to soft peaks in a food processor and sift in the almonds. Spread on a silicone paper-lined baking sheet (roughly 20 x 20cm/8 x 8in) and bake until golden and firm to the touch, about 8–12 minutes.

Melt 50g (⅓ cup) of the chocolate with the butter. Crush the crispbreads and mix them, along with the chocolate hazelnut spread, into the melted chocolate.

Melt the remaining milk chocolate in a bowl set over a pan of simmering water, making sure that the base of the bowl doesn't touch the water. Whip the cream to soft peaks and mix with the melted chocolate to create a smooth mousse.

To build the wagon wheel, spread the chocolate rye mix over the base sponge and chill in the freezer until cold and firm, about 30 minutes. Then, using the round shallow moulds, cut out rounds, making sure to push through both layers as you do so.

Fill the moulds on top of the base with the chocolate mousse, all the way to the top. Level it off using a palette knife and return to the freezer until solid. These can stay in the freezer for a maximum of a month.

When ready to serve, remove the moulds (if you have one, use a blowtorch to briefly blast the moulds, making them easier to remove) and place the wheel back in the freezer until ready to finish.

Melt the chocolate mirror glaze and completely coat the wheel over a wire rack, saving any excess to pour back over to fill any gaps. Return to room temperature before serving.

MAKES 4

100g (½ cup) egg white, about 3 eggs
100g (½ cup) caster (superfine) sugar
100g (1 cup) ground almonds
250g (1⅓ cups) milk chocolate, chopped
2 tsp unsalted butter
6 rye crispbreads
100g (⅓ cup) chocolate hazelnut spread
200ml (scant 1 cup) double (heavy) cream
500ml (2 cups) dark chocolate mirror glaze (available online and in larger supermarkets)

4 round shallow moulds, about 8cm (3½in) diameter

WHITE CHOCOLATE COOKIE DOUGH

WITH HAZELNUT CRUNCH

Preheat the oven to 170°C (325°F) Gas 3.

Melt the butter, transfer to a mixing bowl and stir in the two sugars. Add the eggs and continue to mix. Tip in the remaining ingredients and mix until the mixture comes together to form a dough.

Divide the dough into 4 individual ovenproof dishes and bake for 8 minutes until the dough has browned on top but is still super moist inside.

While the cookie dough is baking, melt the chocolate hazelnut spread in a pan or in the microwave and add the puffed rice. Mix until well coated.

Serve the cookie dough hot, straight out of the oven. Top with the hazelnut crunch and a scoop of ice cream, then sprinkle a little of the crushed biscuits on the top.

MAKES 4

120g (½ cup) butter
100g (½ cup) golden caster (superfine) sugar
100g (½ cup) soft light brown sugar
2 eggs
250g (1¾ cups) plain (all-purpose) flour
200g (1⅓ cups) white chocolate chips
1 tsp bicarbonate of soda (baking soda)
½ tsp salt
1 tsp cornflour (cornstarch)

HAZELNUT CRUNCH
100g (⅓ cup) chocolate hazelnut spread
100g (4 cups) puffed rice

TO SERVE
4 huge scoops of good-quality pecan ice cream
4 caramelized biscuits, such as Lotus, crushed

This is everything you could ever want in a pudding: hot and cold, sticky, sweet and crunchy – it's a wow every time.

MAMA'S PEACH CRUMBLE WITH

BOOZY APPLES AND CARAMEL CUSTARD

SERVES 6

700g (3 cups) freshly sliced peaches
100g (½ cup minus 1 Tbsp) butter
60g (¼ cup) plain (all-purpose) flour
100g (½ cup) soft light brown sugar
85g (scant 1 cup) porridge oats
   (oatmeal)
1 tsp ground cinnamon

BOOZY APPLES
2 Granny Smith apples
1 vanilla pod (bean)
1 cinnamon stick
3 Tbsp Calvados
50g (¼ cup) caster (granulated) sugar
Freshly squeezed juice of ½ lemon

CARAMEL CUSTARD
600ml (2½ cups) double (heavy) cream
7 egg yolks
200g (1 cup) caster (granulated) sugar
1 Tbsp vanilla extract
1 Tbsp cornflour (cornstarch)

Try making this in advance and leaving it to cool slightly before serving. Change up the booze or fruit to give the crumble your own twist – either way it will be glorious.

Preheat the oven to 180ºC (350ºF) Gas 4.

Arrange the peach slices in an ovenproof dish. Using your fingertips, rub the butter into the flour to form a crumb, then add the sugar, oats and cinnamon. Cover the peaches with the crumble mix and bake for 30–35 minutes or until the top of the crumble is golden brown.

Peel and dice the apples. Split the vanilla pod, scrape out the seeds and add them to the apples along with the pod, the cinnamon stick, Calvados, sugar and lemon juice. Cook until the apples are tender but retain their shape.

For the custard, bring the cream to the boil, reserving just 2 tablespoons for later. In a separate bowl, whisk together the egg yolks, a tablespoon of the sugar, the vanilla extract and cornflour. Once the cream has come to the boil, add a little to the yolk mixture and whisk in. Add the tempered yolk mixture back to the rest of the cream and stir continuously over a low heat while the custard thickens.

In a separate pan make a caramel with the remaining sugar. Heat the sugar gently until it has dissolved and then increase the heat to medium and boil until a warm caramel colour has been achieved. Add the reserved 2 tablespoons of cream to cool the mixture down before stirring it into the custard.

Serve family style at the table – if there is any left over this is great the next day too; however, we never have much left!

FROZEN PB&J (PEANUT, BACON, JAM)

SMORES SLIDER

Some recipes are born from a moment of madness; I guess this is one of those and you'll thank me for it. You'll need to be quick when you assemble everything – make sure the ice cream is extra cold, as the whole slider can collapse if you take too much time constructing it.

Put the raspberries in a small saucepan with 2 tablespoons of the sugar and the lemon juice. Bring to the boil and reduce until thick and sticky. Leave to cool.

Cut the doughnuts in half through their middles.

Turn the tub of ice cream on its side and, using a serrated knife, cut 4 x 1cm (½in) discs, through the container. Remove the ring of packaging from around the discs, put the discs on a metal baking sheet and return to the freezer. (You won't need the rest of the ice cream so transfer it to a suitable container and devour when needed.) Find a cookie cutter that is a similar size to the doughnut and cut circles from the 4 ice cream discs you have made.

Start building the slider. Place the bottom of the doughnut on a plate and spoon on some of the cooled raspberry jam. Add an ice cream disc and a piece of maple bacon. Top with two toasted marshmallows and the top of the doughnut.

Be superfast with this one as the ice cream will melt quickly – suppose that means you're just going to have to eat it faster.

MAKES 4

1 punnet (tray) of raspberries
2 Tbsp caster (granulated) sugar
Freshly squeezed juice of ½ lemon
4 sugared jam doughnuts
1 x 500ml (1 pint) tub of peanut butter
  ice cream
4 rashers (slices) of maple-candied
  bacon (see page 24)
8 marshmallows, toasted

RUM-GLAZED ROASTED PINEAPPLE

WITH COCONUT ICE CREAM

If desserts could hug you back, I would be first in line with this one. It's rich and sweet but as light as a feather. Glazed pineapple is magical and takes the flavour to a different level.

For the ice cream, pour the coconut milk, cream and milk into a saucepan. Split the vanilla pod and add it to the pan with the desiccated coconut. Bring to the boil, then leave to steep for half an hour.

Mix the egg yolks with the sugar. Strain the vanilla pod and excess coconut out of the warm coconut mixture and pour the liquid back into the pan. Temper the yolks by mixing them with a few spoons of the warm liquid, then pour this into the pan. Cook over a low heat until the mixture thickens and coats the back of a spoon.

Cool the mixture and churn in an ice cream maker until set. Store in the freezer.

Remove the core from the pineapple quarters and cut each piece into three. Heat a frying pan (skillet) with the sugar and a splash of water and cook until you get a golden caramel. Add the pineapple and the rum, taking care in case the rum causes the caramel to flame up. Once any flames have died down, add the butter. Cook the pineapple in the caramel until deep in colour, and sticky.

Pile into a bowl with some crushed ginger biscuits and a huge scoop of coconut ice cream. Finish with a grating of lime zest.

SERVES 4

1 pineapple, peeled and cut into quarters
200g (1 cup) caster (granulated) sugar
50ml (scant ¼ cup) spiced rum
25g (1½ Tbsp) butter

COCONUT ICE CREAM
1 x 400ml (14fl oz) can of coconut milk
250ml (1 cup) single (light) cream
300ml (1¼ cups) whole milk
1 vanilla pod (bean)
65g (scant 1 cup) desiccated (shredded) coconut
6 egg yolks
135g (⅔ cup) caster (granulated) sugar

GARNISH
Ginger biscuits (cookies), crushed
Lime zest

IT'S
5 O'CLOCK
SOMEWHERE
RIGHT?

With or without alcohol, it doesn't matter what day of the week it is or what time it is, you can rest assured that it is 5 o'clock somewhere!

LOTUS DREAM

Take 4 biscuits and sandwich them together in pairs with a generous amount of biscuit spread.

Add the remaining 8 biscuits and the rest of the biscuit spread to a blender along with the milk and ice cream and process until smooth.

Pour an unhealthy amount into a glass and devour with the biscuit sandwich.

SERVES 2

**12 speculoos biscuits (cookies),
   such as Lotus**
5 Tbsp speculoos spread, such as Lotus
200ml (scant 1 cup) whole milk
6 large scoops of vanilla ice cream

TRIPLE CHOCOLATE MALT DYNAMITE

Blend all of the ingredients together in a blender, adding a little more milk if it's looking too thick.

Pour into a glass and stack everything else on top, finishing with the whipped cream and chocolate sauce, if using.

MAKES 2

6 scoops of chocolate ice cream
200ml (scant 1 cup) whole milk
4 Tbsp Horlicks (malted milk powder)
A large handful of Maltesers

TOPPINGS
There are no rules here – be as
   imaginative as you like! We like to use:
Cookies
Doughnuts
Mini ice creams
Extra Maltesers
Malted milk biscuits (cookies)
Chocolate popping candy
Whipped cream
Chocolate sauce

BERRY CITRUS SOUR

MAKES 1

Ice cubes
50ml (¼ cup) Amaretto
25ml (5 tsp) freshly squeezed lemon juice
25ml (5 tsp) cloudy apple juice
25ml (5 tsp) sugar syrup
1 Tbsp egg white

TO GARNISH
Orange slice
3 raspberries
1 packet of raspberry popping candy

GLASS
Whisky tumbler

Fill a whisky tumbler with ice cubes to chill.

Pour all the remaining ingredients into a cocktail shaker and dry shake (no ice).

Add ice cubes to the shaker and wet shake (with ice).

Double strain slowly into the tumbler ensuring a frothy top.

Garnish with a slice of orange and the raspberries and sprinkle with the popping candy.

CHERRY ALMOND ICE CREAM FLOAT

MAKES 2

2 Tbsp black cherry compote
6 scoops of vanilla ice cream
2 x 250ml (237ml) bottles of cola
Whipped cream
2 x 25ml pipettes filled with Amaretto (optional)
2 packets of raspberry popping candy
2 cherries, to garnish

GLASS
Highball

Spoon a tablespoon of cherry compote into the bottom of
a highball glass and add 3 scoops of ice cream to each glass.

Remove the lid from the bottle of cola. Hold the glass at an angle and wedge the cola bottle into the ice cream. Stand it up, making sure the cola stays inside the bottle, and leave until the cola has emptied out.

Add the whipped cream and the boozy pipette, if using. Sprinkle with the popping candy and throw a cherry on top.

DIRTY BACON MARTINI

For the bacon-infused vodka, preheat the oven to 180°C (350°F) Gas 4.

Lay the bacon on a baking sheet and bake in the oven for about 15 minutes until turning golden. Remove from the oven, brush with the maple syrup and return to the oven for another 10 minutes until nicely glazed. Leave to cool.

When the bacon is cold, push 4 of the rashers into the bottle of vodka and leave to infuse for 24 hours.

Fill a martini glass with ice cubes to chill.

Fill a cocktail shaker with ice and shake the bacon-infused vodka, olive brine and vermouth until blended.

Remove the ice from the martini glass and strain the martini from the shaker.

Finely dice 2 of the olives and place in a small pile on the remaining rasher of caramelized bacon. Skewer an olive through the bacon and arrange on top of the glass to serve.

MAKES 1

Ice cubes
50ml (¼ cup) Bacon-infused Vodka (see below)
1 Tbsp brine from jar of green olives
2 tsp dry vermouth

BACON-INFUSED VODKA
5 rashers (slices) of bacon
3 Tbsp maple syrup
1 bottle of vodka

TO SERVE
3 pimiento-stuffed green olives

GLASS
Martini

MARSHMALLOW CHOCO LUX

Toast the jumbo marshmallow on one side and stick the toasted side to the base of the coupe glass.

Add ice cubes to a cocktail shaker along with all the other liquid ingredients. Shake thoroughly until the outside of the cocktail shaker becomes ice cold.

Double strain and pour into the coupe around the toasted marshmallow.

Using a blowtorch, carefully toast the top of the marshmallow. Add a sprinkling of cocoa powder for a finishing touch.

MAKES 1

Jumbo marshmallow
Ice cubes
50ml (¼ cup) chocolate Irish cream
   liqueur
25ml (5 tsp) Irish cream
25ml (5 tsp) hazelnut liqueur
25ml (5 tsp) honey syrup
Cocoa powder, to garnish

GLASS
Cocktail coupe

HONEY BEE
OL' FASHIONED

Add a couple of ice cubes to the tumbler with 25ml (5 tsp) of the honey Bourbon. Stir thoroughly for around 30 seconds then add 2 dashes of angostura bitters and 1 ice cube.

Stir again for another 30 seconds. Add the remaining honey Bourbon and 1 tablespoon of honey syrup.

Add more ice cubes until in line with the rim of the glass and stir again thoroughly for 1 minute.

Add a small splash of apple juice and stir one last time. Garnish with a slice of orange peel.

MAKES 1

Ice cubes
50ml (¼ cup) Tennessee Honey
   Bourbon
Angostura bitters
Honey syrup
Apple juice
Orange peel, to garnish

GLASS
Whisky tumbler

BUFFALO
BLOODY MARY

MAKES 1

50ml (¼ cup) vodka
25ml (5 tsp) Buffalo Sauce
   (see page 175)
Worcestershire sauce
Freshly squeezed lemon juice
Ice cubes
Pure tomato juice
Celery salt
Black pepper

TO GARNISH
Celery stick
3 cornichons
1 cherry tomato, halved
3 olives
Fresh red chilli
Crispy bacon rasher (slice)
25ml pipette of Buffalo Sauce
   (see page 175), optional

GLASS
Small glass cocktail jug

Add the vodka, buffalo sauce and 2 dashes of Worcestershire sauce to a cocktail shaker. Add a teaspoon of lemon juice and dry shake (no ice).

Fill the cocktail jug with ice, pour all contents from the cocktail shaker over and fill with pure tomato juice. Add a shake of celery salt and black pepper for seasoning.

Garnish with a long celery stick, cornichons, tomato halves, olives, red chilli and a caramelized rasher of bacon.

Add an additional pipette of buffalo sauce for extra goodness, if you feel like it!

#StaySaucy

Sauces and condiments are the icing on the cake, the cherry on top. Mix them up or swap them around – do whatever you like and give several of them a try to find your ultimate combo.

From the hottest of chilli sauces to the coolest of ranch mayos, this chapter is going to have you dousing everything and anything you can in one of these bangers.

1. Roasted Sesame Dressing

MAKES 500ML (2 CUPS)

400ml (1¾ cups) mayonnaise
250g (scant 2 cups) black or white
  sesame seeds, toasted
50ml (¼ cup) mirin
25ml (5 tsp) apple juice
1 Tbsp sesame oil
25ml (5 tsp) rice wine vinegar
Salt and black pepper

Put all the ingredients in a blender and blend until smooth and a light grey colour. If the dressing is too thick, add a little water to loosen.

Pass the dressing through a sieve to remove the sesame seed husks. Season and use as required.

Store in the fridge in a closed container and use within 5 days.

2. Shanghai Sauce

MAKES 500ML (2 CUPS)

200ml (scant 1 cup) dark soy sauce
200ml (scant 1 cup) light soy sauce
100g (6 Tbsp) honey
100g (½ cup) soft dark brown sugar
50ml (¼ cup) sesame oil
100ml (scant ½ cup) rice vinegar or distilled vinegar
½ head of garlic, roughly chopped
50g (scant ½ cup) fresh root ginger, peeled and
  roughly chopped
Bunch of coriander (cilantro) stalks, chopped
Bunch of spring onions (scallions), white ends
  only, roughly chopped

Combine all of the ingredients in a saucepan and bring to the boil. Once bubbling, remove from the heat and leave to sit for as long as possible – this sauce is great if made the day before!

Strain into a suitable container and close. Store in the fridge and use within 7 days.

3. Buffalo Sauce

MAKES 500ML (2 CUPS)

300g (10½oz) fresh cayenne chilli peppers
200ml (scant 1 cup) white vinegar
1 tsp garlic granules
1 tsp onion powder
2 tsp smoked paprika
75g (¾ cup) cornflour (cornstarch)
250g (1 cup plus 2 Tbsp) butter
100g (6 Tbsp) honey
Salt

Chop and blend the chillies to a pulp with the vinegar and 125ml (½ cup) water. Add the spices and cornflour and continue to blend until smooth. Transfer the sauce to a saucepan and slowly bring to the boil, taking care to remove any impurities that bubble to the top.

Remove the saucepan from the heat. Chop the butter into large chunks and slowly blend into the sauce using a stick blender. Once all the butter has been blended into the hot sauce, strain through a sieve to remove any pulp.

Adjust the taste with the honey, adding a little at a time until the desired sweetness is reached, and add salt if needed.

Store in the fridge in a closed container and use within 7 days.

4. Chilli Coconut Satay Sauce

MAKES 500ML (2 CUPS)

1 shallot, finely chopped
Small piece of fresh root ginger, peeled and chopped
1 garlic clove, finely chopped
1 fresh lemongrass stalk, finely chopped
½ fresh red chilli (more if you like it spicy)
2 Tbsp vegetable oil
2 tsp Madras curry powder
1 x 400ml (14fl oz) can of coconut milk
50ml (¼ cup) dark soy sauce
150ml (⅔ cup) sweet chilli sauce
200g (scant 1 cup) crunchy peanut butter
Salt and black pepper

Sweat the shallot, ginger, garlic, lemongrass and chilli in the oil in a small pan until soft. Stir in the curry powder and add the coconut milk.

Add the soy sauce, sweet chilli and peanut butter. Bring to a simmer and then remove from the heat.

Season with a little salt and pepper.

Store in the fridge in a closed container and use within 3 days.

4

5

6

5. Bone Marrow Butter

MAKES 500G (2¼ CUPS)

200g (7oz) bone marrow melt
300g (1⅓ cups) butter
2 Tbsp honey
Black pepper

Bring all ingredients to a simmer in a pan. Remove from the heat and whisk until pale and cool. Season to taste then transfer to a serving dish and keep cool until ready to use.

Store in the fridge in a closed container and use within 3 days.

6. Ko Phan Bang Sauce

MAKES 500ML (2 CUPS)

1 fresh lemongrass stalk
2 kaffir lime leaves
3 Tbsp dark soy sauce
400ml (1¾ cups) sriracha
2 Tbsp sesame oil
100ml (scant ½ cup) white wine vinegar
200g (⅔ cup) honey, plus extra to taste
150g (¾ cup) caster (granulated) sugar
3 Tbsp freshly squeezed lime juice
Salt and black pepper, to taste

Bruise the lemongrass and place in a saucepan with the lime leaves. Add the remaining ingredients and bring to the boil. Remove from the heat and leave to infuse for at least an hour or as long as you have.

Strain the sauce through a sieve to remove the lemongrass and lime leaves. Adjust with a little extra seasoning or honey, if needed.

Store in the fridge in a closed container and use within 7 days.

7. Regret It in the Morning

MAKES 250ML (1 CUP)

4 shallots, chopped
3 garlic cloves, chopped
Small piece of fresh root ginger, peeled
 and chopped
Oil
400g (14oz) fresh red Scotch bonnet chillies, stems
 removed (wear gloves, these are seriously hot!)
 and roughly chopped
250ml (1 cup) distilled white vinegar
100g (½ cup) palm sugar
Salt and black pepper, to taste

Sweat the shallots, garlic and ginger in a little oil until soft. Add the chillies to the saucepan with the vinegar and sugar. Cook until soft, cool slightly and then blitz with a stick blender. Season as required.

Store in the fridge in a closed container and use within 2 weeks.

8. Blue Cheese Sauce

MAKES 400ML (1¾ CUPS)

100g (3½oz) Stilton
100g (3½oz) Roquefort
300ml (1½ cups) mayonnaise
3 Tbsp sour cream
½ tsp celery salt
½ tsp black pepper

Combine all the ingredients in a blender and blend until you reach the desired consistency.

Store in the fridge in a closed container and use within 3 days.

10

11

12

13

9. Mushroom Ketchup

MAKE 125ML (½ CUP)

25g (1 cup) dried porcini
1 white onion, chopped
250g (3¾ cups) chopped chestnut mushrooms
250g (4 cups) chopped portobello mushrooms
Oil
60ml (¼ cup) malt vinegar
2 Tbsp dark brown sugar
2 Tbsp Worcestershire sauce
Freshly squeezed juice of ½ lemon
1 Tbsp soy sauce
Salt and black pepper, to taste

Soak the porcini in warm water until rehydrated, then drain, discarding the liquid.

Sweat the onion and mushrooms in a little oil until soft. Add the drained porcini and continue to cook. Add the vinegar and sugar and reduce until the vinegar has evaporated.

Remove from the heat and allow to cool slightly, then blend with a stick blender. Season with the Worcestershire sauce, lemon juice and soy sauce, and salt and pepper to taste.

Store in the fridge in a closed container and use within 3 days.

10. Slow-Roasted Garlic Mayo

MAKES 500ML (2 CUPS)

3 heads of garlic
1 Tbsp olive oil
A few sprigs of fresh thyme, leaves picked
2 Tbsp crème fraîche
400ml (1¾ cups) mayonnaise
Freshly squeezed juice of ½ lemon
A good pinch of salt

Preheat the oven to 170°C (325°F) Gas 3.

Remove the top of each head of garlic. Place on a large sheet of foil and drizzle with the oil. Scatter the thyme leaves over the top. Wrap in the foil and bake until soft and brown, about 40–60 minutes.

Add everything else to a blender and squeeze in the garlic, discarding the skins. Blend until smooth.

Store in the fridge in a closed container and use within 3 days.

11. Burnt Onion Jam

MAKES 250G (1 CUP)

4 white onions, unpeeled
2 garlic cloves, unpeeled
Olive oil, for drizzling
100g (½ cup) soft dark brown sugar
100ml (scant ½ cup) balsamic vinegar
Salt and black pepper

Preheat the oven to 190°C (375°F) Gas 5.

Halve the onions and crush the garlic, leaving them all in their skins. Drizzle with oil and add a little seasoning. Cook in the oven for 35–40 minutes, or until the onions start to catch and char around the edges.

Allow the onions and garlic to cool and then squeeze them out of the skins onto a chopping board. Chop to a pulp and add to a saucepan with the sugar and vinegar.

Bring to the boil and reduce until dark and sticky.

Store in the fridge in a closed container and use within 7 days.

12. Buttermilk Ranch

MAKES 500ML (2 CUPS)

300ml (1½ cups) mayonnaise
100ml (scant ½ cup) sour cream
100ml (scant ½ cup) buttermilk
2 garlic cloves, chopped
50g (1 cup) freshly chopped dill
100g (2½ cups) freshly chopped chives
Freshly squeezed juice of ½ lemon
Salt and black pepper

Mix all the ingredients together well, seasoning to taste.

Store in the fridge in a closed container and use within 3 days.

13. Everything Sauce

MAKES 125ML (½ CUP)

3 Tbsp tomato ketchup
4 Tbsp mayonnaise
2 Tbsp American mustard
A dash of Worcestershire sauce
1 Tbsp chopped shallot
2 Tbsp chopped gherkins
1 Tbsp freshly chopped chives
Salt and black pepper

Mix all the ingredients together and season – then throw it on everything!

Store in the fridge in a closed container and use within 3 days.

Bread and Butter Pickles

SERVES 4

300ml (1¼ cups) apple cider vinegar
150g (¾ cup) caster (granulated) sugar
¼ tsp celery seeds
2 Tbsp mustard seeds
¼ tsp fennel seeds
¼ tsp dried chilli (red pepper) flakes
500g (18oz) mini cucumbers
1 white onion

Put the vinegar, sugar and 100ml (scant ½ cup) water in a saucepan and bring to the boil. Remove from the heat, add the spices and infuse while you cut the cucumber into 5mm (¼in) slices, and thinly slice the onion. Add the cucumber and onion to the pickling liquid and refrigerate overnight.

Store in the fridge in a closed container and use within 1 week.

Quick Pickled Cucumber

SERVES 4

¼ cucumber
1 tsp white sesame seeds
2 Tbsp rice vinegar
1½ Tbsp caster (granulated) sugar

Cut the cucumber in half lengthways and scrape out the seeds with a teaspoon. Slice on the diagonal and mix with the sesame seeds, vinegar and sugar. Refrigerate and leave to pickle for at least 20 minutes. Drain before using.

Store in the fridge in a closed container and use within 3 days.

Fig and Bacon Jam

MAKES 500ML (2 CUPS)

200g (1⅓ cups) dried figs
150ml (⅔ cup) apple juice
1 banana shallot, finely chopped
2 rashers (slices) of smoked bacon, finely chopped
1 garlic clove, finely chopped
Light olive oil, for frying
100ml (scant ½ cup) balsamic vinegar
75g (⅓ cup) soft dark brown sugar
1 cinnamon stick
2 cloves

Soak the figs in the apple juice until soft, then remove and chop. Retain the liquid.

Soften the shallot, bacon and garlic in a pan with a little oil. Add the vinegar, sugar, spices and figs then bring to the boil and reduce by half. Add a little of the apple juice soaking liquid and continue to reduce until thick and sticky.

Allow to cool. Remove the cinnamon stick and cloves before serving.

Store in the fridge in a closed container and use within 3 days.

Chorizo Jam

MAKES 225G (1 CUP)

150g (scant 1⅓ cups) chorizo, diced
2 shallots
1 garlic clove
2 Tbsp brown sugar
75ml (⅓ cup) red wine vinegar

Sauté the diced chorizo over a medium heat in a frying pan (skillet) with the shallots and garlic. Once soft, add the sugar and vinegar and reduce until sticky.

Store in the fridge in a closed container and use within 3 days.

Zaatar Tahini

MAKES 200G (SCANT 1 CUP)

100g (⅓ cup) tahini
75ml (⅓ cup) freshly squeezed lemon juice
1 garlic clove
25g (5 tsp) zaatar

Simply blend all of the ingredients, except the zaatar, together with 100ml (scant ½ cup) water, then stir in the zaatar at the end.

Store in the fridge in a closed container and use within 3 days.

Roasted Garlic Houmous

MAKES 500G (2 CUPS)

Head of garlic, plus 1 garlic clove
2 Tbsp olive oil, plus extra for drizzling
1 x 400g (14oz) can of chickpeas (garbanzo beans), drained
Freshly squeezed juice of 1 lemon
60g (scant ¼ cup) tahini

Preheat the oven to 170°C (325°F) Gas 3.

Drizzle the head of garlic with a little olive oil and wrap in foil. Bake for about 40–60 minutes, until deep and golden.

Add the remaining ingredients to a food processor along with 50ml (¼ cup) water and blitz until smooth. Add a little extra water at the end if needed to adjust the consistency. Squeeze in the roasted garlic cloves, discarding the skins, and give a final blend.

Store in the fridge in a closed container and use within 3 days.

INDEX

189

INDEX

ACKNOWLEDGEMENTS

This page introduces the Wingmans Hall of Fame, along with our loyal customers without whom we would not be where we are today!

Starting with our family who have put up with us and been by our side since Day 1. Housing us, clearing up after us, letting us use their home kitchens and garages as prep and storage facilities, assisting with logistics, last-minute emergencies, blood, sweat, tears and everything in between. We love you all:
Jeffrey Turofsky, Mark "The Farge" Ford, Amanda "Wingmama" Turofsky, Kim Milton, Zacharie Turofsky, Paige Ford, Jay Turofsky, Rita "Bubi" Laurier, Helen "Oma" Grunberg, Leonard "Grumps" Laurier, Sue Arnold, Tyson, Oscar

Now these guys are the ultimate wingmen and wingwomen. We would not be where we are today without them – the original wing squad, through thick and thin we salute you all:
Adam Horwood, Christian "DJ BBQ" Stevenson, Joshua Lipschitz, Nathan Pomerance, Scott Kreiger, John Clarke, Liam Chau, Jamie Leigh-Chau, Michael Michalaki, Daisy Webster, Dominic Berko, Stephen Moses, Joshua Ungar, Liz Norris, Charlotte "Cheffy" Kemp, Anthony Gregson

Once we'd developed the initial menu and brand artwork, we were finally ready to rock and roll! The next step was to find somewhere we could set up shop to test out our products and start creating brand awareness.

The list of event/festival partners, trader managers and all the incredible individuals and businesses we have collaborated with over the years is endless. They have always supported the Wingmans brand, welcomed us with open arms and provided us with the opportunity to serve our wings at some of the most iconic venues, festivals and events. I will say it again: the list is endless but if you are reading you know exactly who you are and

we hope to work with you all on exciting projects for years to come. Special thanks to Billie and Denise Chandler and Nathan Kosky for hosting the first ever Wingmans experience!

We are extremely lucky to have an incredible team of wing technicians working with us that have helped prep, cook, toss, sauce and garnish every portion of wings served. Their talent and creativity when it comes to food are second to none and we are extremely lucky to have them as a part of our family. Wingmans prides itself on the quality and consistency of its products and we are forever grateful to have such an incredible team of chefs with us that share the same passion and love for food as we do. Special thanks to these superhero individuals who have been a core part of all our kitchen and food operations:
Filippo Scantamburlo, Connor Leggatt, Paulino Corpuz, Ellen Da Rocha, Danielli Esteves Da Silva, Sam Njenga, Sundip Malhotra, Vernon Williams, Lloyd Brackett

Now some of these guys are no longer with the brand but we will never forget the levels of exceptional service they have provided to ensure that every one of our loyal customers has the best Wingmans experience, time and time again. Setting the standards high, big love goes to:
Chiara Maffia, Selin Yetismis, Faisa Ahmed, Joshua Tobi Oke, Zoran Prica, Zachary Evans, Laura Amigo Salcedo, Sophia Soso Jasmine

Aaaaaannnnnnnd last but not least the incredible Quadrille guys who have made this book dream a reality and who have been patient and put up with us throughout this incredible book journey:
Céline, Katherine, Dan, Carole and Sophie, Rebecca, Sinead, and all the sales, publicity and marketing teams.

David & Ben

PUBLISHING DIRECTOR
Sarah Lavelle

**SENIOR COMMISSIONING
EDITOR**
Céline Hughes

SENIOR DESIGNER
Katherine Keeble

PHOTOGRAPHER
Dan Jones

FOOD STYLISTS
Carole Hector, Sophie Hammond

PROP STYLIST
Rebecca Newport

HEAD OF PRODUCTION
Stephen Lang

PRODUCTION CONTROLLER
Sinead Hering

Published in 2020 by Quadrille,
an imprint of Hardie Grant Publishing

Quadrille
52–54 Southwark Street
London SE1 1UN
quadrille.com

Text © David Turofsky and Ben Ford 2020
Compilation, design and layout © Quadrille 2020
Photography © Dan Jones 2020

Cataloguing in Publication Data: a catalogue record for
this book is available from the British Library.

ISBN 978 1 78713 500 0

Printed in China